THE
BEST ROADS
OF
CALIFORNIA

A Guide For
The Automobile &
Motorcycle Enthusiast

The Best Roads of California
A Guide for the Automobile
& Motorcycle Enthusiast

Copyright © 1988 by Larry Blankenship

Published by
RoadTales Publishing
P.O. Box 30218
Long Beach, CA 90853

Cover Design: RoadGraph
Cover Illustration: Paul Huntoon

Printed in USA

First printing, 1988

ISBN 0-942841-01-8

THE
BEST ROADS
OF
CALIFORNIA

A Guide For
The Automobile &
Motorcycle Enthusiast

By Larry Blankenship

ROADTALES

CONTENTS

CHAPTER 4

CHAPTER 5

ACKNOWLEDGEMENTS

There have been numerous people and organizations who have helped me through this project:

My best friend, Paul Huntoon, whose friendship and loyalty is matched only by his ability to keep me out of Mexican jails. Also, my cohort, Bobby Hardison, whose ideas and encouragement were invaluable, plus extra kudos to him for keeping The Shark running.

Thanks go to my great friend, Ross Tillman, for his support. My driving gloves are off to Tim Eggert for giving me a job when I needed one. Special thanks go to Bill and Kathie Miller for having faith and believing in me.

In addition, a big thanks go to my dear Mom and Alyce for their enduring patience. Also a tip of the cap to Vivian the Burrito Queen, Donna the Wordsmith, Kathleen Marusak, Debbie Pietsch, Captain Walt, Lei, Ross J., Ruth, Dana, Karen Glazener, The Great Sepetini Brothers ("Look, no net, no net..."), Nigel Condor, Dodds Book Shop, Talking Heads, Mark Isham, Mexican road builders, Pacifico Beer Co., Rusnak Porsche, Panama Joe's, Dr. Roberts, Dr. Ferrari, California Microcomputer Rentals and my nutritionist at Taco Bell.

Also my heartfelt thanks go out to the automobile and motorcycle enthusiasts who gladly shared their special roads and highways with me.

Finally, I could not forget the person who, in their infinite wisdom once said, "Nothing easy ever shows how good you are."

May you all find your own special road...

Dedicated to
The Shark

VIN# 0940EN463998

Wheels at the end of the tunnel...

HEY, READ THIS FIRST

I consider this book a celebration of fun roads. But like any *good* celebration, it requires a bit of organization . . .

I'm a firm believer that travel on great roads should be long enough to enjoy not only the driving and riding experience, but also provide sufficient time to appreciate the roadside scenery. So accordingly, a minimum of 25 miles was set for a road to be considered for this guide. That leaves out many of the short urban blasts that crisscross California's sprawling communities; and even though some of these quick dashes can rival the best roads in this guide, the soul of this book is as much about the *open road* as it is about discovering exciting, challenging pavement.

I've tried to strike a balance between providing you with practical, nuts-and-bolts information, i.e., distances, driving times, elevations, etc., yet give you a sense of each road's unique traits and temperament. Much of what makes a road enjoyable to travel is found deep within its contours—and in the way those contours interact with the surrounding landscape and terrain. For that, a detailed engineering analysis seemed completely inappropriate. (That would be akin to relying on degrees of angle to describe a beautiful woman's looks.)

The first two chapters cover a range of topics of interest to both the first-time visitor and the seasoned California traveler. In addition, you'll find the criteria I've used to rate each road, plus information on everything from the California Highway Patrol to an overview of popular California maps.

For those who find time and distance important considerations, you'll find basic information at the start of each road's summary; all times and distances listed are one way and tend to be conservative. The direction (east, west, etc.) used for each summary is also noted.

Keep in mind that Mother Nature can close a road in a blink of an eye, and a road's condition can quickly change due to temporary road work. Also, the CHP—a most flexible organization—can step up patrol of an area in response to everything from a public outcry to an increase in accidents. But thankfully, this stellar collection of high performance roads changes little (except for venerable Highway 1) each year.

A potpourri of helpful information awaits the enthusiast in the Appendix of this road guide. (I don't know about you, but I've yet to warm to the idea of naming any section of a book after a damn body part.) You'll find a list of states that have a pact with California to accept information on any of their licensed residents who receive moving violations during their stay in California.

The Appendix also includes the regional phone numbers for the California Highway Information Network (CHIN), a helpful, but under-used telephone service that provides regularly updated information on road and travel related conditions throughout California. A listing of stretches labeled with a 65 mph speed limit is provided too, since any lengthy travel in California will probably include time on this state's rural Interstates.

Though this guide comes complete with a map highlighting California's best roads, its whimsical nature better reflects my own sense of humor than an accurate portrayal of each road's course. Anyone motoring these roads will find their travels greatly enhanced by having a good map close at hand since many of the best stretches are keyed to small towns and hamlets. (As mentioned, Chapter 2 contains a brief review of some of the more popular California maps.)

*　　　*　　　*

Anytime someone lists their opinion of the best, they're invariably going to leave out someone else's best. The fact that many fine roads didn't make the final cut of 25 is sure to sadden—even anger—some enthusiasts. Please feel free to let me know what *you* think.

You see, the idea that there's still a couple of winding, slippery passages hidden in some corner of this marvelous state—with descriptions so inviting that they immediately have me planning a trip in their direction—well, that's a thought that *more* than appeals to me. Because, for the serious enthusiast, there *really* are only two kinds of roads: Fun roads, and the roads you use to get to the fun roads.

CHAPTER 1

WHAT MAKES A GREAT ROAD?

I've written this guide to the best roads of California using six criteria:

Degree of challenge
Quality of scenery
Congestion
Road condition
Level of patrol
Sense of fun and adventure

Degree of challenge

In this guide I've tried to include roads that reward the skilled driver and rider. Roads capable of utilizing (if you so choose) all of the capabilities inherent in an automobile or motorcycle. Roads that not only challenge your abilities, but *enhance* them too.

It's here, out on these two-laners, that the enthusiast can find any level of challenge he or she desires. Take them hard, at a pace that will have the best drivers and riders traveling with quickened pulses. Or take them easy, providing you and your passengers with a leisurely tour of some of the best roadside scenery California has to offer. It's entirely up to you. I've tried to accommodate both attitudes, though I must admit that my approach is purposely slanted towards the heart-thumping ride.

Traversing most of these roads requires a high level of concentration on your part—no matter what your driving attitude. It's the kind of concentration rarely called upon in your day-to-day driving. Know and respect your limits and abilities, as these roads can tire you quickly, both mentally and physically.

Another reason why a book like this is long overdue is the vehicles themselves. Automobiles built today are safer and easier to drive than those built just a few years ago. For the car enthusiast it has been an exciting renaissance. With increases in horsepower coupled with improvements in aerodynamics and suspension design, today's automobiles are not only quicker, but also handle better than their predecessors. In addition, modern tire technology can upgrade the roadholding ability of any car.

Changes in motorcycle design have been even more dramatic. In the last few years, a whole new class of high performance motorcycle has emerged that's geared towards the sporting enthusiast. With an abundance of horsepower and much-improved handling, these sport-bikes have taken the aggressive rider to dizzy new heights of pleasure. Improvements in aerodynamics and tire technology—similar to those in the automobile world—make this new breed of motorcycle a thrill to ride.

Though I took to these roads using a variety of automobiles, I'm sure it comes as no surprise that I preferred using high performance vehicles. On the other hand, good scenery can be savored no matter what kind of transportation you use. But for the most of us, there is an additional level of enjoyment and appreciation that comes with taking the open road in a well-suspended, reasonably fast automobile or motorcycle.

Scenery

Living and traveling throughout California for over 25 years has not lessened by wonderment at the beauty and variety that this state offers. Though easily the most populated state, its roads take the traveler to landscapes that remain pristine and unspoiled.

This collection of roads can introduce you to places in California that are rarely equaled elsewhere in breadth and beauty. Follow this guide and you'll find roads coursing through lush green forests and towering redwoods. Seaside routes which cut along wind tousled cliffs are well represented here, too. You'll find routes passing through landscapes so harsh and desolate, that little can openly survive on their hot, sun-baked surfaces. And if your interests are in great, beautiful wilderness areas with snow-capped mountains feeding cool, gurgling streams, you'll also find pleasure with many of the roads in this book.

Yet, the draw of the urban corners—where man's imprint has a high profile—has not been ignored either. Those traveling to Los Angeles, San Francisco, San Diego (and most other major cities in California), will find in this guide twisting, winding, *inventive* roads that'll whisk you away from the hustle and bustle; out towards the secluded valleys, meadows, and mountains that make California such a wonderful place to be.

The golden state is also blessed with a vast array of geology and plant and animal life. Our diverse climatic regions create a kind of "melting pot" for a wide range of plants and trees. Few places can match the variety of foliage found within the boundaries of California.

Our animal life is no less interesting with California being home to life that's both large and small, hearty and frail. You'll find the burly black bear foraging in the higher elevations contrasted by the graceful Monarch butterfly, migrating in the winter to the protection of the eucalyptus groves hugging the central coast.

To me there is something quite wondrous about a state crossed with roads that start you in the still-cool desert at morning, towards towering forests by lunchtime, passing through fertile farmlands in mid-afternoon, placing you at the white-capped Pacific Ocean, just in time to enjoy one of our California sunsets.

Congestion

This is a real pet peeve of mine. I hate roads with a lot of traffic. I can get all I want in any large city in California. I wanted roads where travel could be accomplished with a minimum of fuss and congestion. Most of the highways summarized here meet that goal.

While researching this book, I traveled at different times and days, enabling me to find out how bad the traffic could get. You'll be pleasantly surprised to know that most of the roads in this guide remain relatively free of traffic, even during the busy summer months. Where applicable, you'll find a notation in each summary mentioning any area of potential or probable congestion.

Road condition

You'll find all of the roads in this guide to be in reasonably good condition. There are no bumpy, potholed dirt roads in this guide. Oh, we've got plenty of them in California. (Though some joke that California's worst roads are now the aging, battered freeways criss-crossing the Los Angeles area.) But most of us wouldn't traverse dirt roads in high performance autos and motorcycles—instead preferring smoother, better behaved pavement. Occasionally, you'll drive through road repair work in progress that feels like a shock absorber testing ground. But I assure you all of these roads are easily driven (barring mother nature and disasters, of course) by any automobile or motorcycle in good condition.

I drove several roads that met many of the criteria established for the roads in this guide—except they were in serious need of repair. We'll keep an eye on these highways and their repair schedules. If, and when, they're improved, we'll consider including them in the next edition of our guide and newsletter.

Patrol

Nobody enjoys getting a ticket. Any road that was a meeting place for cops didn't get in this book. Any road with even a hint of a speed trap isn't here. Driving in California over the years, I've come to the simple conclusion that the smaller the road, and the further away from civilization you are, the less likely you are to encounter someone with the authority to give you a citation.

The majority of the roads in this guide are lightly patrolled. You'll find comments notating any situation to the contrary. Please don't interpret this as meaning that the authorities will never grace these highways—I promise you they will. It's just my way of saying that the odds are much greater for ticket-free driving on the roads featured in this guide than on the Interstates. In my mind, luck plays too large of a role in who gets caught and who doesn't. Hopefully, this guide will put a little of that luck in your glovebox.

Fun and adventure with people

Over the years, these roads have provided me with some great adventures (most printable, a few not). All of these two-laners rank high in the fun-to-be-on category. They've also given me the chance to meet many of the warm and kind people who live and work in the small towns tucked along the way.

I think that rather than get out there for themselves, many people writing about travel in California rely a bit too much on dull and boring Chamber of Commerce tourist brochures for information. Much of this material is silly and self-serving, i.e., "The Annual Pumpkin Valley Dead Stick and Donkey Festival is world-renowned for it's great food and all-star entertainment..."; or, "The Harrysburg Desk Drawer Museum treats the whole family to a fascinating look at the history of desk drawers since time began...". I wouldn't plan *my* vacation on this stuff.

There are so many books that suggest where to stay, where to eat, where to sightsee, where to do this and that, that I have purposely stayed away from these topics, instead concentrating on the roads. On occasion, I mention a place of business simply because I and my friends have enjoyed it over a long period of time. I did not accept *any* freebies in the course of writing this guide. I don't know about you, but I get angry when I read descriptions that turn out to be very different from what the place is really like. Makes you wonder who's getting rich, doesn't it?

Fun and adventure with things

Things are buildings, places, sites, things you see lying on the ground but don't dare touch, and stuff like that. These can be a lot of fun too. In this guide you'll find descriptions of normal things like picnic spots, but I also refer to some of the more odd and weird places I've stumbled upon while researching these highways; power stations that look like they're out of an old Frankenstein movie, or the infamous "squirrel slalom" stretch of one back road. I've also tried to include brief descriptions on a range of sights and scenery along each road that might incite a bit of fun—whether they be mountains, towns, or businesses.

Each of these highways offers you a variety of interesting, sometimes offbeat things to look at and ponder. Unlike our Interstates, these less traveled roads make it easy for you to get out of your car, or off your motorcycle, and enjoy things. And I like that.

CHAPTER 2

DRIVING
IN
CALIFORNIA

Driving safely

My first driver's training was in the tenth grade when I was fifteen. It consisted of driving around the suburbs of San Diego with two other students and a gym teacher who seemed more interested in the football game that weekend than teaching us about driving. Our vehicle was a big brown Dodge with automatic transmission; the dreaded "STUDENT DRIVER" slogan plastered on the roof and three sides of the car.

The big Dodge also had a second brake pedal on the passenger side for our teacher. This was in case we forgot our instructions about braking before we hit something. The teacher would explain various rules and traffic laws as you and your fellow students took turns driving around town. And, of course, no driver training course would have been complete without being forced to view movies featuring car accidents so graphic in their depiction of auto injuries, that you never wanted to drive again! Looking back now, I doubt that my driver's training course played much of a role in making me a better driver as an adult.

When you think about it, most people acquire the bulk of their driving experience going to and from work, running errands—often using the same roads with the same terrain, scenery, and traffic patterns. It's this type of driving that can erode the driving skills often needed on the roads in this book. Many people faced with an emergency maneuver don't have the foggiest idea what to do, or how their vehicle will behave.

So maybe, just maybe, I have some of you wondering how you can become a better driver. Fortunately, there are numerous qualified organizations and schools that, by providing a combination of classroom and track time, can help you improve your driving skills in just a few hours. That may sound expensive, but let me assure you that from my own experience, it doesn't have to be.

My driver education began on a clear and warm Saturday morning one summer. The event was a one day driver's school sponsored by the Porsche Owners Club and Beverly Hills Porsche & Audi. It was held at Willow Springs Raceway, a challenging nine turn course located about 70 miles north of Los Angeles. Using the desert floor and the adjacent foothills for territory, it's often used for automotive and motorcycle testing. It was there that I got a chance to operate my vehicle near its limits, in a controlled environment, with the emphasis always on *safe* driving.

Many sceptics might think this was just a bunch of crazy drivers careening their expensive toys around a race track. Well, that's an incorrect assumption. My morning began with classroom training by a skilled instructor. We covered everything from passing techniques to basic car control—all with an emphasis on controlling your vehicle through a wide range of maneuvers.

Next, we moved to an observation point overlooking the track, above turn four. Here we received additional input and guidance from our teacher, using the vehicles in front of us to illustrate valuable information and techniques.

After a brief safety inspection of my automobile, I was brought into the pre-grid area before entering the track. But, I still wasn't driving at this point—I was in the passenger's seat. Strapped into the driver's seat was a highly skilled instructor who specialized in my model of car. Since he knew the course and my model of automobile (I found out later that he was closing in on the track record in this class), he was able to give me plenty of tips about the course and how it related to my car's handling characteristics.

Even before I drove one foot on that track, I had learned more about driving in a few short hours than many people learn in a lifetime. I understood for the first time what having *control* of a vehicle really meant. I learned about weight transfer, constant radiuses, transition states and a wide range of conditions, actions, and techniques that can help drivers control their automobile in an emergency situation.

I also gained an acute awareness of just how important it is to be constantly aware of your surroundings, other vehicles, road and weather conditions, and a myriad of potential problems you might encounter while on the road. Driving the same roads day in and day out can erode the capacity to concentrate. How many times have you been cruising along in your day-to-day driving only to suddenly realize that you can't remember anything about the last five minutes of driving? There are two things that will make you a safer driver: the ability to concentrate and the knowledge of how to control your vehicle in an emergency situation.

If you want to improve your driving skills, join a local car club that sponsors driving and training sessions. You'll find many car clubs advertising in the classified section of most auto magazines. These one or two day driving sessions can be surprisingly inexpensive. (My session cost just $20.) If you want a more detailed and personalized course— and have the time and money—there are a number of good driving schools who hold driving courses in California. I've listed some of the best in the Appendix.

No section on driving safely would be complete without mentioning drinking and driving. DON'T DO IT. If you think it's okay just "once in a while" you could be dead wrong. In California, over 1,500 men, women, and children die every year due to someone drinking and driving. If you insist on drinking while you drive, I hope you get caught, go to jail, lose your license, and get your insurance raised. We don't need drunk drivers on the road. If you're going to drink, then please don't drive.

California Highway Patrol

These people are simply the best at what they do. I have always found this state's Highway Patrol to be a courteous, knowledgable, and professional group of people (with more than a few serious enthusiasts among their ranks). Over the years, I've received a ticket or two from the CHP and they've always been fair with me, occasionally saving me bucks by writing a lower speed, or if the reason was reasonably plausible, even forgoing the ticket entirely. They patrol many of the roads in this guide, so you're likely to see them as you travel.

Much has been written about what to do if you get pulled over for a traffic violation. Considerable amounts of money have been made by companies offering enthusiasts a variety of books and videos exploring various methods and techniques for avoiding tickets. One of these might be a wise investment if you find speeding tickets piling up on your record faster than old newspapers in a corner.

If you do see flashing lights in your mirror, try to remember a few guidelines that will help ensure that you don't anger the officer before you've had a chance to plead your case. When you see lights behind you, move to the right as soon as you can (using your turn signals). Stop on the shoulder with all wheels off the road. You've at least shown that you can pull over like a pro. Hopefully, the officer won't think that the reason you are so proficient at this is because you've had a lot of practice.

At this point, there are two schools of thought on how to deal with the possibility of getting a ticket. The first says, do it with honor; admit your infraction and take your medicine like a man. The second method is to say, do, or try just about anything to get out of your ticket. I've always had good luck using a policy of honesty, though, I must admit to being guilty to adding a bit of color or emotion when I felt that it would help my case. ("Really officer, a giant space ship caught me in some kind of tractor beam, taking control of my vehicle! No shit?...72 in a 55? Boy, some beam, huh?")

A few years back, the CHP was having problems keeping up with high performance vehicles that often traveled the roads in California at, well, what would be described as a bit beyond the speed limit. Many of these fast machines (oh, the stories I've heard) could easily leave the overweight and underpowered Ford and Dodge police cruisers far behind. Consequently, in many areas of California, you'll now see eight cylinder, five-liter Ford Mustangs wearing the fabled CHP insignia. In fact, they're already on their second generation of these fast cruisers, and most of the officers I've talked to love driving these hot Fords.

10

The CHP does not currently own any radar equipment of their own. In fact, they are the only statewide police force in the country that doesn't use radar on its highways. Unfortunately, there's a catch: they *will* use radar for speed limit enforcement if it's supplied to them by local authorities—and at last count that was the case in 19 counties, though their patrol is often sporadic, and should be of little concern to the enthusiast traveling the roads in this book.

In California, few enthusiasts own radar detectors since radar is rarely used to enforce the speed limit on most main highways and Interstates. In the Golden State, local authorities—who are free to use it on any chunk of pavement that's in their local jurisdiction—write most of the speeding violations clocked with radar.

Over the years, the CHP has tried to convince the California legislature to approve the purchase of radar equipment, though the CHP points out that, technically, they already have that right. But the CHP feels that it's such a sensitive subject with Californians that they would prefer to have the politicians approve the purchase—and thus take much of the public's wrath for what would surely be an unpopular move. So far the California legislature refuses to acquiesce, continuing to leave radar equipment out of the budget.

But the CHP has other weapons in its arsenal. The most cunning method is the use of spotter planes to catch speeders. The technique is simple: using a fixed-winged airplane, potential violators are timed as they move between painted timing lines of a fixed distance. Those significantly exceeding the speed limit have their vehicle's speed and description radioed to black-and-white ground units waiting patiently for the unsuspecting speeder.

It's an efficient ticket-writing system—often corralling two or three vehicles at a time. I hate it. But rest easy, you won't see any CHP planes on the small back roads making up much of this road guide, it simply isn't cost effective for the CHP to use them on lightly traveled roads. Instead, they concentrate their aerial show along the main arteries, including Interstate 5 and Highways 50 and 101, among others.

One of the features of our newsletter/magazine, *California Driver,* is a column noting the most popular stretches and times for the CHP spotter planes. It will be updated every issue using reader input plus our own staff's observations.

The CHP got the okay from the California legislature to use unmarked cars for the first time starting in January 1987. The vehicles lost the distinctive black and white color scheme normally associated with CHP enforcement vehicles. The only noticable marks on these cars are the words "HIGHWAY PATROL" in small print on the doors. This test program was initiated to combat the dramatic increase in the number of traffic accidents involving big rigs, and is set to run for one year, though I wouldn't be the least bit surprised to see it extended.

The CHP has assured all who will listen that the unmarked vehicle program will only be used to track down big trucks speeding up and down California's main highways and Interstates. I have a funny feeling that the CHP will try to expand this program, including smaller prey in its scope. If that's the case, hopefully, cooler heads will prevail.

Maps

It's pretty much unanimous that the Automobile Club (AAA) maps are the best. They are accurate, highly detailed, and easy to read. The one drawback is that you have to be a member of the Auto Club to get them. Once you are a member, however, all the maps are free. Membership for the first year is about $50. I'm a member because they offer a wide range of services including towing, travel planning, and car registration. They also seem to have offices everywhere in California, and I like that.

If you are inclined to buy maps as you travel, there are several good ones available. A company called Thomas Bros. Maps makes a fine atlas of California highways and city streets, called the California Road Atlas & Drivers Guide (available at most large drug stores). I'm not sure that you'll need this much detail, but take a look and decide for yourself. Some people use this comprehensive guide for all their travel needs in California, and at about $17 a copy it's a bargain. One drawback to the Thomas Bros. map book is that no mileage figures are available on the individual map pages. Instead, you're left with a one page, down-and-across chart for figuring mileage—and then only between major cities.

Another good series of maps is produced by Murray's, though at a $1.50 a pop, it can get expensive if you're traveling extensively. (Something tells me that's what Murray's had in mind.) I'm not a real big fan of the popular Rand McNally maps sold in many motels and gas stations. I do like and use their big USA Road Atlas, but I find their individual state and city maps more difficult to read and follow. They also seem to be updated less frequently than some of the other maps for California. They've recently come out with a deluxe version (read: more money) that's easier to use.

Another product, The Sunset California Freeway Exit Guide, was released in 1986 by a company out of Carlsbad, California. At first glance, it seems like one of those wonderful once-in-a-lifetime ideas: a guide to all the gas stations, restaurants, lodging, and just about everything else that sits off each exit of major freeways in California.

Unfortunately, many will find this guide a bit too cumbersome to easily use. I've watched numerous friends try to quickly (the key word here is quickly) find places to eat and gas up, only to give up in frustration. And using this exit guide while driving requires a second person who must patiently get through the 300-plus pages of maps, exits, explanations, and numerous cross references.

In addition, how many of us traveling solo take the time to plan hours and miles ahead exactly where we're going to eat or gas up? (Or go shopping? Yes, it even lists major department stores sitting off of each exit.) Often pulling off at a new exit or town can lead to a fun and interesting discovery. But, I guess on the other hand, how many looking for food would take an exit knowing that the only restaurant waiting for you goes by the name of Porky Bob's Meat Parlor and Restaurant? ("Honey, I don't think I'm all that hungry just right now.")

It should be interesting to see if the people who compile this guide are willing to invest the time and money needed to keep this guide up to date. In California, what was a gas station on Monday can easily become a flower store on Tuesday. I picked up my copy for four bucks at a book store, a steep discount from the ten buck retail price—usually not a good sign for a new publication. Still, it can be a wise investment for those traveling extensively on the major freeways in California.

California speed limits

California has something called a *Basic Speed Law*. And its meaning is quite simple: you must never drive faster than is safe for the conditions present at the time. If that statement doesn't strike you as having a lot of meaning, well, read on.

According to California's Department of Motor Vehicles driver handbook, the speed limit can be affected by a wide range of factors, including: the number of other cars on the road, their speed, and even the road surface. Keep in mind that this is all regardless of what the *posted* speed limit is on that road. The bottom line is that a driver could (but in reality, rarely) get a ticket for driving 45 mph in a 55 mph zone, if it was deemed to be too fast by a police officer. This would make a lot of sense if the fog was so dense that you couldn't see beyond the dashboard. So as you can see, our *Basic Speed Law* does make sense after all!

And yes, a few stretches of desolate California Interstate have finally been labeled with a 65 mph speed limit. (You'll find a listing of all 65 mph stretches in the Appendix.) The sound of discontent with the 55 mph speed limit grew from a mumble to a roar that few politicians dared ignore. Lack of compliance was rampant, not only in California, but everywhere in America. Good, decent, law-abiding people were being turned into criminals by this unenforceable federal statute.

On rural Interstates like California's I-5, slow lane speeds were frequently in excess of 65 mph. Anyone crazy enough to attempt travel at the double-nickel on desolate stretches of I-5 was creating a traffic hazard, plain and simple. Thankfully, few motorists dared travel at 55 mph on these lonely sections (probably out of fear for their own safety, more than anything else).

Many police organizations, including our own California Highway Patrol, had recommended that the speed limit be raised on California's Interstates running through rural areas. And with these super highways constructed with a 70 mph speed limit in mind, few changes were necessary other than to replace the speed limit signs. The early returns released by the CHP are encouraging, showing a drop in fatalities on the California Interstates with increased speed limits. Hopefully, as drivers and riders become accustomed to having a 65 mph speed limit, additional sections of California highway will get more reasonable speed limits.

California drivers

I refuse to believe that California drivers are *that* much different from those in other regions of America. We may have a bit more than our share of skilled drivers, but, alas, we also have our share of drivers with habits that can make driving hazardous: plenty of leftlane bandits, cars with immobilized turn signals, and generally inept drivers of all ages and either sex. Of course we have plenty of drivers who think darkness is an appropriate time for fog lights—even when there is no fog. (They are called *fog lights,* aren't they?)

But I think that, overall, most drivers in California are courteous and knowledgable. And despite a rash of media hyped freeway violence in the summer of 1987, most drivers in California give up the right-of-way easily, rarely embarking on the territorial battles that can ensue when two vehicles approach decreasing road space. People driving in California for the first time might feel that the drivers around them are more aggressive than back home, but even that, I think, is at times questionable.

I remember a few months back, easing onto a crowded Southern California freeway—behind the wheel was an old friend from the Midwest, visiting me on his vacation. He remarked that the "crazy California driver" running on his tail certainly didn't belong on the road. At the first opening in traffic, this "California driver" roared by, sporting Texas license plates. My friend, needless to say, grew very quiet. After a few weeks of traversing the Los Angeles freeway system, he learned to respect the ballet-like precision at which the locals travel the freeways.

Californians and their cars

We in California love fine vehicles. We lust after, and will do just about anything (including the ever-popular living-beyond-your-means technique) to get a fine road car or motorcycle parked out front. A friend of mine jokes that driving a fast, beautiful, well-suspended automobile in California is like having a great tan: you don't really need it—but you sure look and feel better having it. And, you know, he's right. The California enthusiast loves fine vehicles, and unabashedly so.

The California enthusiast is a knowledgable consumer well informed on many of the latest vehicle developments. Yet, we rarely take things *too* seriously; we're able to laugh at such diverse (some might say *perverse*) items as fake cellular phone antennas, blow-up doll passengers and convertibles stuffed with six-foot teddy bears, complete with bowtie and RayBans.

Californians, thankfully, see no reason why a sense of humor need stop at the driveway. Happy motoring!

CHAPTER 3

BEST
ROADS
OF
SOUTHERN
CALIFORNIA

Angeles Crest Highway

Direction: East.
Distance: About 60 miles.
Driving time: Two to three hours.
Congestion: Light to moderate.
Road condition: Good, but rocky in spots.
Patrol: Light to moderate.

Angeles Crest Highway, well known to the locals, can be a helluva fun road to drive and ride. Much of this journey finds Angeles National Forest teaming up with the San Gabriel Mountains to provide the traveler with plenty of great, big scenery through L.A.'s original skyscrapers. When coupled with this mountain path's numerous fun driving and riding opportunities, you begin to understand why this road is often thick with two and four wheeled enthusiasts.

Angeles Crest Highway, rising into the mountains, is often used to reach the winter ski resorts nestled in these mountains. That, of course, means that Angeles Crest Highway qualifies as a fun road only when it's not covered with ice or snow. In the winter, tire chains are often required in the higher elevations of Angeles Crest Highway. Our narrative will deal exclusively with warm weather experiences on Angeles Crest Highway.

On most warm weekends you'll have plenty of company on this road. Many of your motoring companions will be indulging in that age-old ritual of tread removal by aggressively exploring the adhesion limits of their vehicles. For years this has been the favorite proving ground for members of the frenzied driving and riding club. (Though you'd be surprised at how much you can learn by following one of these road warriors through the rocky canyons.) Anyone attempting to deal with this road's mischievous ways at anything over nine-tenths effort is in for quite an education. Driving in a crowd on Angeles Crest Highway can be an intense, and at times, unnerving experience.

This highway starts out in one of Los Angeles' bedroom communities—La Canada; a well-to-do place snuggled in the Verdugo foothills. You'll find Angeles Crest Highway originating at Foothill Boulevard, the main street running east-west through La Canada.

Angeles Crest Highway starts in a northerly direction, meandering easily for about two miles through a quiet residential area. The fun begins with a quick, curving upward ascent. On a clear day (yes, there are clear days in Los Angeles) the first few miles provide spectacular vistas of the hodgepodge of cities that make up the San Gabriel Valley.

Once into the mountains, you'll be transported on a road containing a wide range of curves and twists—many blind. Traffic can bottle up in the section leading up to the Clear Creek Info Center. There are a few passing zones, but usually they aren't long enough to allow everyone waiting to pass to do so. These passing lanes can provide some scary moments when impatient motorists attempt to claw their way to the front of the pack in their quest for open road.

Many people coddled by guard rails, medians, and curbs are surprised when they get on a mountain road like Angeles Crest Highway for the first time. On much of this highway, steep cliffs—minus guard rails—are often just a few feet from your tracks. Sheer drops—measured in the *thousands* of feet—are par for the course on mountain highways that follow the contours of the land like this one does. Angeles Crest Highway is a fine example of the philosophy of building a road around Mother Nature's curves—not through them—making for better driving and riding, plus, leaving the surrounding landscape looking as natural as possible.

As Angeles Crest Highway begins to move in an easterly direction, you're in for mile after mile of exciting bends and esses with plenty of wicked curves lying in wait. If you're looking for low-g sweepers, you've come to the wrong place. Instead, you'll find a roving, serpentine highway full of elevation changes. You'll quickly climb to over 4,000 feet by the 12 mile mark. On warm days, you should keep an eye to the temperature gauge, especially if you're running in the higher rpm ranges.

You'll also find the air getting thinner. Turbos will be right at home in these higher climbs. Folks with normally aspirated engines will not be so fortunate. As engines begin to gasp for oxygen that's increasingly harder to come by, you'll feel a slight loss of horsepower. At Dawson Saddle, near the 45 mile mark, you'll get up to an ear-popping 7,901 feet before finally curving downwards.

You'll encounter several wide, u-shaped turns that let you view the asphalt just traveled or preview the pavement that's waiting. Several of these turns allow views into deep rock canyons that are both breathtaking and alarming. As you venture between the Shortcut Ranger Station and Charlton Flats, you'll find a fun batch of esses waiting for you. There's even a store for food and drink a few miles past Charlton Flats, making this highway feel almost civilized. A mixture of pine trees and chaparral join with the rocky terrain to make this section of the course beautiful, yet sparse looking.

You'll drop about 2,000 feet in elevation on the 13 miles between Cloudburst Summit and the small village of Wrightwood. Traffic picks up considerably going in and out of Wrightwood, so you might want to turn around and head back towards L.A.; though if you're hungry, this mountain town offers plenty of dining options.

Our trek concludes about four miles past Wrightwood, at the junction of Highway 138. This final jaunt is made up of straight, uninspiring road, with moderate to heavy traffic. But I suggest you take a few minutes to drive the last few miles and catch the interesting changes in the ecosystem on the back side of the San Gabriel mountains. Just moments after leaving Wrightwood, you'll find cactus and yucca trees replacing hearty mountain pines. No less impressive is how this mountain range affects the weather pattern—effectively making these last few miles a desert run.

Imbedded into the San Gabriel Mountains, Angeles Crest Highway provides a great mountain workout using a delightful combination of curves and hooks sure to keep your reflexes busy. With rugged mountain forests rising all around you, the views are often just short of spectacular. My favorite section for scenery is coming down from the Dawson Saddle summit area, around Dorr Canyon. And at these elevations, you'll usually find patches of snow on the ground—even in the warm months.

Many automobile and motorcycle publications use this road for vehicle testing and reviews, and it's easy to understand why. Its close proximity to Los Angeles, matched with its high scores in the fun-to-drive category, have made this a reliable passage over the years. Generally its reputation is well deserved. But, I have a few reservations about Angeles Crest Highway.

First, the rock slide problem gets worse every year on this road. And that's dangerous in my mind. Coming around blind curves—even at what would be considered a slow pace—you'll occasionally be forced to make quick direction changes to avoid the numerous small rock slides. Unfortunately, the road is so narrow in places that the only place to go to avoid tire damage (or worse) is into the oncoming lane. Again, not a safe situation. The last time I drove Angeles Crest Highway, I had just shelled out big bucks for a new set of high performance tires. So maybe I was a little too paranoid, but it made me nervous to play slalom with the rocks strewn across the road. That's just not my idea of a good time.

Second, there's the traffic. Plenty of resorts and campgrounds translate into a lot of campers and trailers on the road. And, anyone who has had the unfortunate experience of following one of these rolling townhouses up a mountain highway knows first-hand how little practice these drivers get between vacations.

Third, on sunny weekends, it seems like very 16 year-old car jock with more than two cylinders and a gallon of gas finds his way up to this road. All seem to drive older, poorly maintained cars shod with cheap, pseudo-performance tires emblazoned with raised white letters that shout out names like "Go Like Shit 60's" or "Spin-Kings." Hey, give me a break. A congested mountain highway is not the place to learn that your car does not have the handling capabilities of the cars in the auto ads on TV. The California Highway Patrol evidently agrees—as you'll often see them out in force on weekends, especially on the first half of this highway.

On the other hand, you'll also encounter drivers and riders possessing a goodly amount of skill—coursing this capricious mountain path in a variety of modern, high performance autos and sportbikes. Numerous turnouts allow for socializing or enjoying the scenic overlooks.

My last reservation about Angeles Crest Highway has to do with a little road called Angeles Forest Highway. Reviewed just a few pages from here, it lies to the east—hiding in the shadow of Angeles Crest Highway's reputation.

I think Forest Highway is the more fun of the two roads. It's got plenty of challenging pavement, yet none of the debris and obstacles that often mar Crest Highway. Plus, you'll find little traffic on Angeles Forest Highway, even on the busiest of weekends. And as long as amateurs continue to terrorize Crest Highway, you'll see little in the way of black-and-whites on the Forest Highway. Scenery is the only category that Crest Highway wins.

Your best bet is to get up on Angeles Crest Highway on a weekday. If you're lucky enough to live near this road, I suggest you take a day off from work as the driveability factor of this road improves immensely when traffic is light.

So, the choice is yours. And no matter which highway you choose, you'll come out a winner. Either will produce miles of pleasure. I just hope that not too many of you take my recommendation on little Angeles Forest Highway as I'd love to keep that enjoyable path to myself a while longer.

Angeles Forest Highway

Direction: North.
Distance: About 25 miles.
Driving time: Half an hour to an hour.
Congestion: Light.
Road condition: Good.
Patrol: Light.

"N3"

If you're in the Los Angeles area and have a high performance vehicle, you have a problem. It's called traffic. Traffic during the day. Traffic during the night. Traffic on the freeways and traffic on surface streets. This seemingly around-the-clock congestion can make automobile and motorcycle enthusiasts quite frustrated. Brief bursts of speed on freeway onramps and a few g's here and there on freeway transition roads do not constitute fun driving!

Well, my frustrated driving friends, I offer you relief in the form of two high-spirited mountain roads, Angeles Forest Highway and Angeles Crest Highway. These two routes, running serpentine through the San Gabriel Mountains, lie just north of the Los Angeles Basin, and are easy to get to from any point in Southern California.

The lesser-known of these two is Angeles Forest Highway. I discovered this fine mountain road years ago while looking for a shortcut to Willow Springs Raceway, the well-known track that lies off of Highway 14, near Lancaster. Checking out my large Auto Club wall map, I noticed a small road called Angeles Forest Highway (listed as N3) running off of famous Angeles Crest Highway. On the map, Angeles Forest Highway appeared shorter and quicker than my normal freeway route.

So, running out of time and expecting the worst, I headed north through the snooty community of La Canada towards Angeles Crest Highway (listed as Highway 2 on many maps). After traveling about ten miles on Angeles Crest Highway, I found the small Clear Creek Info Center on the right side of the road. A left turn at the intersection where this tiny info booth sat brought me to the start of Angeles Forest Highway.

And, what did I find? Oh, just a supurb two-lane mountain road that's guaranteed to impress even the most jaded of road enthusiasts. This road dishes out every kind of lucious twist and turn that you could want. And on top of that, it delivers it all in a compact, easy to handle 25 miles!

Our route runs entirely within the confines of the Angeles National Forest. This beautiful, yet often desolate national reserve is home to a variety of recreational activities including camping, hiking, and hang gliding. I'm not sure that Angeles Forest Highway traverses the most lovely section of this forest, but you'll find several terrific views as Angeles Forest Highway cuts across mountain slopes, chaparral-covered canyons, and deep ravines.

Angeles Forest Highway begins with a slow left-handed sweeper that tells you right off that this is a special piece of road. You'll start with two lanes on your side of the line—all the better to quickly pass anything that might have an idea of keeping up with you. You'll have less than a mile to handle your passing duties.

The first 20 miles of Angeles Forest Highway dole out just about every kind of gravity-defying act that you can experience in a car or on a motorcycle. Its path swoops, swirls, and curls through some fairly steep canyons, delivering an amazing array of curves and bends. Yet, it's a road that instills confidence rather than fear—even for the novice. Oh, there are a couple of decreasing radius curves that quickly separate the men from the boys—but on the whole it's the kind of run that offers something for the expert and novice alike. Ready and waiting to provide the enthusiast a wide range of basic thrills, Angeles Forest Highway screams out to be driven hard. No bustling traffic, it's lightly patrolled and well maintained too. Folks, this is one impressive road.

Except for an occasional curve speed sign, there are no posted speed limits on Angeles Forest Highway. And, like most mountain roads, the edge of the pavement is usually just inches away from your tires. But, surprisingly, this mountain road lacks any steep, laborious climbs. Instead, it starts as an easy, upward path, then moves slowly downward near the end. Even on hot days, properly maintained engines shouldn't have a problem with overheating.

Angeles Forest Highway presents a different personality in the last five miles, changing from a path draped with curves and esses to one consisting of long, high speed straights. The transition begins at about the 20 mile mark with a mile and a half straight that's in good shape except for a few minor repair patches. Those stuck with the old 85 mph speedometers (a dumb idea if there ever was one) can only guess at how fast you could go on this tempting straight.

On the remainder of this spin you'll find the road made up of additional—though shorter—straights, broken up by an occasional bend or curve. It's as if the creators of this road figured that after 20 miles of fabulous twists, a few well-engineered straights—allowing for nearly flat-out motoring—would be the perfect finale to this fine mountain road. There's certainly no shortage of fun on the remaining few miles of this fine chunk of asphalt.

Angeles Forest Highway spends much of its life slicing through rugged mountains, creating a most agreeable path as it moves towards its conclusion in the high desert. The surrounding landscape becomes increasingly desolate as you nibble around the edges of the desert that binds these mountains to the east. Clear days will allow for visibility far out into the rugged desert lands. And though the views on the last few miles aren't exactly postcard material (the best scenery lies on the first half, in the more mountainous region), I think the wonderful driveability of this highway more than compensates for the lack of travel brochure scenery.

Another advantage of Angeles Forest Highway is its great condition. As this road unfolds, you'll find the surface in uniformly good condition. Few problems exist with falling rock or other debris that often plague other mountain two-lanes.

There's little evidence of civilization on Angeles Forest Highway. On the last few miles you'll probably spot a few mail boxes; fronting a collection of old beaten-up houses, their neglected yards a foot deep in weeds. This road also embraces more than one old truck carcass, littering the landscape, looking like momentos to a more useful time. All in all, there's little to distract the enthusiast from the task at hand.

At the end of this spin, you'll be out in the middle of nowhere. The community of Palmdale sits about five miles away, offering plenty of places to eat if you aren't too picky. But the nice thing about this highway is that it's short enough so that after a brief rest, you can turn around and tackle it again. Or even better yet—let a friend try his or her hand at this marvelous chunk of highway. As Angeles Forest Highway winds back towards Los Angeles, the asphalt becomes progressively more challenging, gently easing any anxiety that a first-timer might have about driving this road.

If ever there was a recipe for a pure driving road, all of the ingredients could be found on Angeles Forest Highway. This is a highway built for enthusiasts—and for many it represents an irresistable lure. If you're within driving distance of this road, and you aren't looking for your keys right now, I suggest you cancel your car magazine subscriptions, throw this book away, and start shopping for a used yellow Chevette with a buzzy AM radio and broken window cranks....

Ortega Highway (Hwy 74)

Direction: Northeasterly.
Distance: Approximately 28 miles.
Driving time: Usually less than an hour.
Congestion: Moderate.
Road condition: Average.
Patrol: Light to moderate. Occasional radar.

Orange County is a delightful place to live or visit. It has a great climate, wonderful people, and more amusement parks than you could ever hope to visit. But wait, there's more. Prowling along Orange County's Pacific Coast Highway offers the chance to view up close some of the finest automobiles in the world. Every kind of rare or exotic high performance vehicle you've ever dreamed about is likely to reside in one of the exclusive, yet informal beach communities that dot the Orange County coastline. (The Newport Beach area is a favorite of many.)

But where do you go in Orange County if you're up for some good driving or riding fun? Well, now for the bad news. All the great roads in Orange County are about gone now, except for Ortega Highway. (And we had to cheat at that, with the last few miles running through Riverside County.)

Ortega Highway (no one calls it Highway 74) leads you from the coastal foothills, through the mountainous Cleveland National Forest, and then drops you quickly into Elsinore Valley, home of pretty Lake Elsinore. For the enthusiast it combines plenty of sporting road with fine scenery in a drive that can be wrapped up in less than two hours. And though not in the class of an Angeles Forest Highway, this road provides those in Orange County a good forum for winding out those exotic cars and swift sportbikes.

Our journey begins at the intersection of Interstate 5 and Ortega Highway, in the community of San Juan Capistrano. Heading in a generally straight, northeasterly direction, the first two miles pass through a pleasant high-income neighborhood. Unfortunately, with an initial speed limit of 40 mph, the first few miles won't come close to satisfying any yearning you might have for first-class entertainment.

It would be easy to give up on Ortega Highway in the early

going as the meager scenic diversions consist of a nursery or two and a few fields where growing corn is the main attraction. But as you begin to leave the housing tracts and bustling business parks behind—picking up speed in bits and pieces—the scenery starts to improve. You'll also notice the road taking on a slight incline as Ortega Highway begins to wind its way towards a summit nearing 2,700 feet.

For the first ten miles you'll motor through chaparral covered foothills as the mountainous Cleveland National Forest looms ominously ahead. In the early miles the road is a recipe of easy curves blended with hilly straights, with few of the straights long enough to safely pass slower traffic. On occasion I've seen speeds approaching 100 mph on this part of Ortega Highway—though often the level of traffic won't safely allow you to travel at those speeds. (On the average day this road sees about 14,000 vehicles.)

After teasing you for ten miles with snippets of fun asphalt, Ortega Highway finally begins to put its best foot forward. Passing the San Juan Hot Springs turnoff (about 12 miles out) means that *serious* fun is about to begin in earnest. From here on, the asphalt offers numerous samples of twisty mountain terrain surely built with high performance vehicles in mind.

Ortega Highway veers into Cleveland National Forest with a vengeance, carving its way through a series of canyons, making a course that provides mile after mile of deliriously good driving. With switchbacks battling esses for supremacy, sporting types will need plenty of concentration to keep up with this thrilling mountain trail. At the higher elevations, steep drops—looking like scenery for old B-movie car crashes—are a constant companion. Ortega Highway gets downright cantankerous when boxed in by the steep walls of rock. It fights back using a narrow path that leaves little room for shoulders, turnouts, or errors.

This highway is full of tricks. The 15 to 25 mile leg is easily the most challenging and treacherous stretch. Mountain roads are notorious for odd banking and camber; you think you've got just the right amount of steering input and here comes five *more* degrees. Ortega Highway seems to have an example of every oddball curve ever engineered into a highway. And, needless to say, I think well-suspended motorcycles and automobiles will be right at home on this squiggle of a road.

Unfortunately, the road's surface is not nearly as impressive as its contours. The surface can be rough in places. especially after a rainy winter. Overall I'd rate this road's condition about average.

Heading towards Lake Elsinore, you'll often encounter plenty of oncoming traffic consisting of an assortment of campers, pickup trucks, and vehicles trailering boats. Getting my vote for the worst driver award on this winding road are the people behind the wheels of the numerous small pickup trucks. They seem to constantly drive either right up to, or just beyond, the limited handling ability of their little haulers. On some of the steeper ascents, I've seen guys traveling so fast as to not only need all of their lane, but also five feet of yours. You've been warned.

The last few miles down into Elsinore Valley offer the enthusiast some tantalizing thrills not unlike those encountered while downhill skiing. Again, steep cliffs act as constant reminders that you can't be too careful on this final, dizzy descent. These last few miles are almost totally devoid of guardrails. And the ample supply of off-camber twists and turns helps keep the true enthusiast busy as the road hurtles you downwards, streaking from one wicked corner to the next.

The most spectacular views on Ortega Highway are on the steep run that sends the traveler scurrying down into Elsinore Valley. Unfortunately, it's often difficult to pull over since this road's crooked ways often make it near impossible to preview much of the upcoming pavement for turnoffs. But stopping at one of the few cliffside vantage points will yield great views of this picturesque valley, which sits in a region known as the Inland Empire.

Our other source of scenery, the Cleveland National Forest, often takes a backseat to the impressive road that cuts through it. Full of forests and near-barren rocky canyons, it often gives the impression of being a hostile place. But, all in all, I find its desolate beauty attractive.

In contrast, sections of Elsinore Valley are definitely not my idea of great zoning laws at work. Though there are some pleasant looking areas in the community of Lake Elsinore, much of the valley looks like a mish-mash of trailer parks, dirt roads, and landscaping performed by the blind.

You'll find the patrol sporadic on this highway. Though as we go to press the CHP does not own any radar of their own, they *will* use radar for traffic enforcement if it's supplied to them by local authorities. (For more information on this bizarre situation, see the section on radar in Chapter 2, *Driving in California.*)

But don't be too alarmed. The good news is that, from my experiences on this road, the CHP doesn't use it everyday. And the CHP readily admits that they have no set pattern on when radar is used on Ortega Highway. Of the over 700 tickets written on this highway during the first six months of 1987, about 40% were for speeding citations using radar. (It's actually a pain for the CHP to use radar since their procedures make it a two car process: one to measure the speed, the other to pull you over and handle the paperwork.)

But the level of patrol notwithstanding, I like driving this road. It's close to my home so I'm on it frequently. I wring the most pleasure out of this mountain passage by making my appointment for early Saturday or Sunday morning—before everyone else is out and about. Getting up with the sun ensures a few precious hours of delightful driving. And that's a commodity that's becoming increasingly rare in large metropolitan sprawls like Orange County.

With Orange County's voracious appetite for land, I guess that someday this road will hold little for the serious enthusiast. But for now, it's the best this area has to offer. And for most, this road will deliver a good amount of unabridged driving.

Highway 74

Direction: South, then east and north.
Distance: About 35 miles.
Driving time: Around an hour.
Congestion: Light to moderate.
Road condition: Good to average.
Patrol: Light to moderate.

Highway 74 is an interesting road; though not topping the list of world class driving or riding strips, it offers a good range of terrain and scenery. It's also a road of contradictions as real estate developers grab ever larger chunks of virgin desert land for new housing projects. Fortunately, plenty of open spaces still exist, helping to make much of this journey an unfettered one.

We begin our trek at the junction of Highway 243 (also in this guide) and 74. I start here because this section of Highway 74 offers choice motoring, yet holds little of the congestion that flaws this road in and around Hemet. Portions of the often clogged section running from Highway 215 to Valle Vista could provide good motoring (mainly from Valle Vista east to Highway 243), but congestion and badly timed traffic lights make much of Highway 74 lying west of Hemet a frustrating stretch. Add an endless catch of fast food parlors, cheap motels, and other garish signs of man, and you begin to understand why I prefer to start my travel on Highway 74 at the junction of Highway 243, where Mountain Center is located.

From our starting point at Mountain Center, you'll discover four miles of fine mountain road. Traffic will be light as you head southeast, and that's good as plenty of good driving and riding awaits the enthusiast early on. Within two miles, you'll reach Keen Camp Summit, topping out at just under 5,000 feet.

About four miles out, the mountains move back from Highway 74, creating Gardner Valley, a lovely place blessed with lush green meadows and bountiful stands of pine. This mountain valley allows the road to grab a firmer toehold on the landscape, taking many of the kinks out of the pavement, allowing higher speeds for a time. It's not *too* civilized, mind you, offering just under ten miles of enjoyable pavement, full of little hills that require a firm hand if they're taken at a fast clip. With just the right amount of mountain curves and swerves thrown in, you'll find this stretch pleasurable.

As you cruise through this scenic valley, the distinctive mountain peaks lying to your left are slapped with descriptive names like Cone Peak, Pyramid Peak, Lion Peak, and Bald Mountain—the highest rising just over 7,000 feet. The ragged mountains to your right evidently don't have enough personality to qualify for individual names, instead receiving the collective name of Thomas Mountain.

About 12 miles into this trek you'll pass the turnoff for Highway 371. The next stop is Burnt Valley, where Highway 74 will hike back into the mountains, reaching for another high point, Santa Rosa Summit at 4,919 feet. It's here that Highway 74 begins to require a bit of scrambling to keep up with its contours.

From the summit, you'll begin to head downwards, with the road ever-so-slowly unreeling bits of twisty road. As the mountains again border this road's path, their rocky frames force the pavement into a more sporting personality, making the path an ingenious and satisfying one. You'll have little trouble—except where speed advisories are posted—keeping up with the double-nickel speed limit.

This mountain leg, running from about the 12 mile mark until we reach the outskirts of Palm Desert, will take you on a 20 mile excursion through a variety of landscapes and terrain. Along with a road full of medium-to-tight curves, much of this stretch is built upon hills, providing further incentive for the enthusiast to take this stretch with a bit more intensity. You'll find the tightest curves posted with speeds in the 30-40 mph range, and most are nicely banked, adding to both the pleasure and safety of this cruise. In addition, the pavement on the 12-to-32 mile leg is in good condition.

On the mountainous portions of this trek, gauging traffic is often a hit-or-miss affair. And since there are few passing lanes, it's easy to get boxed in—making traffic seem heavier than it really is. This is a popular weekend route for those from Orange and San Diego Counties seeking out the warmth of Palm Desert.

At about the 20 mile mark, you'll catch a brief glimpse of civilization as you pass through the mountain communities of Spring Crest and Alpine Village. In the warm months, neither looks as nice as their names sound, though in winter they come into their own as pleasant places.

The transition from cool mountain valleys to desolate desert is accompanied to the beat of fast, winding road. Oak and pine mix it up, making it difficult at times to tell where the mountains end and the more remote desert regions begin. But one thing is certain: you'll have much *bigger* scenery now, with views stretching for miles, filling the horizon with rugged desert dioramas. Moving almost exclusively downwards now, you'll find the asphalt in great shape as you cut and slash through rocks, chaparral covered mountains, and who-knows-what-else on a fiesty course towards the desert floor.

From Big Horn Overlook you'll find Highway 74 gets steeper as it now moves in a northern direction. Haphazardly placed guardrails add little security to the last ten miles. The final section of Highway 74 is somewhat dangerous—treacherous even—especially the tricky back-and-forth angles of the swirl of pavement aptly named Seven Level Hill.

Just before you begin your descent, there's a convenient vista point that features a fantastic panorama of the desert floor that you'll soon be traveling through. Get as much sightseeing in as you can here, as the devious descent ahead will require *all* of your attention.

Watch yourself on this tight, downhill course. There's little curve speed advisory information to guide you, and it gets narrow in spots, too. For many, 50 mph in stretches would really be pushing it, as it often feels like a tightly wound race course concocted with too many corkscrews—and too few safety features. Use plenty of caution here as your downward momentum only adds to the danger. (Or the thrill, I guess, depending on how you look at it.) One plus is that most curves are well banked, adding a margin of safety to this angled spiral.

From my experience, this road is usually not overflowing with quality drivers or riders—though you'll see many of the marques that represent luxury and performance. If you're traveling in a crowd, you'll be able to quickly ferret out the skilled driver from the amateur as this section requires more finesse than anything else if you're to accomplish this descent cleanly. With a smidgen of restraint along for the ride, you've got a darn good piece of road that's just waiting to show the talented driver and rider a good time.

Heading down Seven Level Hill exposes the traveler to spectacular views of the surrounding desert floor and canyons. Highway 74, its swirling path cut through the shoulders of steep mountain sides, seems to have been built to afford the best views possible. It's difficult at times to keep your eyes on the road. Though often barren, these mountains are striking in their desolate beauty. After the first autumn rains, many of the desert's beautiful plants bloom, bringing color to a seemingly lifeless-looking area.

You'll finally reach the desert floor via a straight that leads the traveler directly to civilization. The last couple of miles on Highway 74 hold little to interest the serious enthusiast as it courses through

31

the outskirts of the community of Palm Desert. Much of the land along the road is full of contrasts; one moment you'll find the landscape reclaimed by man, full of grassy knolls and swaying palm trees placed just the right distance apart—clearly defining somebody's version on what the desert should look like. But the next block might be untouched desert, desolate, full of shrubs—true to its origins. Beyond this palm-lined street waits a myriad of gas stations, restaurants, traffic lights, and—well, you get the idea.

Coming to an end at Highway 111—a busy intersection in Palm Desert—Highway 74 has taken the traveler on a diverse course through a wide range of scenery, all in less than an hour. That great, tantalizing mecca of the desert, Palm Springs, lies to the northwest, less than 20 minutes away.

If you're planning a trip to Palm Springs from the Los Angeles area, and have a bit of time, you might want to consider including Highway 74 and 243 (also in this guide) in your itinerary. Each is a fine road, neither requiring big chunks of time. Both provide a blend of easy touring with fast, well-banked twisty sections sure to please most enthusiasts.

Highway 74, in its fun, disorderly path through these mountains, makes an aggressive approach seem almost mandatory. Patrol is usually light, though on weekends the second half of this road can get thick with CHP. You won't see the typical direction signs (north, east, west and south) tacked underneath the Highway 74 sign while traveling this road, as no sign budget could afford all of the direction changes this road takes! And that, my enthusiast friends, is a situation that bodes well for anyone seeking serious two-lane adventure.

Highway 78

Direction: East.
Distance: 55 miles.
Driving time: One to two hours
Congestion: Light to moderate.
Road condition: Good.
Patrol: Light.

In California, you can travel from the ocean, to the mountains, and on towards the desert in such a short time that it makes you wonder if Mother Nature wasn't playing favorites when creating the geography we label California. Well, here's a road that introduces you to at least two-thirds of that diverse geographical playground, though if you're willing to take on the envious assignment of starting at the beach for breakfast or brunch, then all three environs— the sea, mountains, and desert—can be yours in a matter of hours.

Beginning deep in pine topped mountain ranges that are surrounded by vast national and state parks, Highway 78 descends swiftly into the arid desert region of the Anza-Borrego Desert State Park. For the enthusiast, it turns in a stellar performance featuring pavement that opens with a winding mountain passage and closes the show with arrow-straight pavement that encourages frequent visits to the thicker part of the speedometer. This path's multiple contours are blessed with several shifts of scenery and terrain, giving Highway 78 a diverse itinerary that's sure to bring a satisfied smile to those who love to drive and ride.

This road begins in the charming mountain community of Julian, an attractive spot just above the 4,000 foot level. Though it's a bit too big, too bustling, to be called a *village*, there's lodging available, plus an ample supply of eating establishments. I usually track down this highway right after the first snow because it provides the California traveler with the rare opportunity to execute some serious maneuvers through beautiful, snow-kissed mountain scenery. (Unless the snowfall is unusually heavy, the road is sure to be open and in good condition.)

Another advantage to wintertime motoring on Highway 78 is the more moderate weather. The cooler temperatures make travel through this road's desert-like second half a safer proposition. Not a bad idea when summer temperatures frequently soar past the century mark by mid-morning—staying there for most of the day. Spring and autumn are the ideal times, bringing cooler climates that allow for travel less harsh on man and machine.

As you begin this trek on Highway 78, you'll travel only a third of a mile before leaving the confines of Julian. Just outside of town, most make the right turn onto Highway 79 (also in this guide), which leads south towards the San Diego area.

With Julian ranking as the highest point on this route, you'll begin to angle downwards soon after leaving the city limits. From there, the enthusiast's initiation to Highway 78 begins via an exhilarating stretch that uses a choice collection of twists and switchbacks to grab your attention. And the scenery doesn't let you down either. Flush with views of mountains blanketed by pine forests, it's a scenic area, whether or not there's snow on the ground.

For the first seven miles—until about Banner—the enthusiast will find a course that displays a delightfully lively temperament. Though not as bent as many mountain runs, this section is outfitted with enough downward lefts and rights to keep you directed to the task at hand. Soon, the steep mountains that first hemmed in this highway move back, leaving you to stream along a dry creek bed. And though you've already descended 1,500 feet in the first seven miles, there's an additional 2,700 feet of occasionally gut-wrenching elevation to drop before reaching the desert floor.

At about the eight mile mark you'll encounter straight road for about three miles. With few moments now left to weave among Alpine woods, this long straight is the first step in the transformation to desert lands. The change takes less than ten miles, going from cool mountain forests to an arid, barren-looking region that, at first glance, gives the impression of being incapable of sustaining life.

The 10 to 25 mile leg features a medley of fine road. Initially the pavement courses along, and just above, the usually dry San Felipe Creek. Varying in width from just a few feet to hundreds of feet across, this winding creek bed cuts an inventive path, forcing the road into a variety of contortions as it ventures onward in an easterly direction.

This section of road renders several straights that should be of sufficient length to allow the passing of slower traffic—further enhancing this road's driveability. You'll also find teams of small hills under foot (wheel?), encouraging the road to make numerous small elevation changes, adding to Highway 78's already high fun-to-drive quotient.

The scenery on the 10 to 25 mile leg reflects the transition from rocky, forested peaks to uninhabited desert. Mountains, looking like they were born out of wedlock from some angry tussle between two mountain ranges, give this area a rugged texture. Pinyon Ridge, the craggy mountain range off to the left during much of this stretch, effectively cuts off the rest of the world, adding desolation to this road's roster of adjectives.

The halfway point lies just west of the Borrego Springs Road turnoff. The second half of Highway 78 is exclusively a desert run, with the mountains flattening, then performing a disappearing act altogether. The remaining pavement can be summed up with two words: *fast* and *straight*. Unlike most of the roads in this guide, few curves or turns wait to alter it's arrow-like path. I'm not recommending that you break the speed limit, but I've seen battered, ancient pickup trucks negotiate this desert at over 90 mph. (And I'm not even going to *hint* at what I've seen modern high performance vehicles travel at along here.)

You'll find few traces of civilization along this lightly traveled route. The only town of substance is Octillo Wells, just past the 30 mile mark. In its parched grasp live about a hundred souls—hardy folks existing with little of the conveniences that you and I take for granted.

On the second half of our excursion, few variations exist in this highway's contours. Only occasional doglegs and a once-in-a-while hill prevent this desert run from heading razor straight into the seemingly endless emptiness of the desert badlands. It's a passage that enables those who prefer to travel at higher speeds the chance to do so. Patrol is extremely light (despite the "PATROLLED BY AIRCRAFT" sign). What patrol there is consists of the CHP, plus the brown and white trucks that belong to the San Diego County Sheriff Department.

Many see the desert as a barren and inhospitable place, having little to offer the traveler. But those with a keen eye will find themselves amidst a vast and intriguing land that's home to hundreds of species of desert plants. Travel this road, and one you're sure to see is the asparagus-like agave, or century plant. Rising up about ten feet, spring time incites its skinny stem to burst out with clusters of bright yellow flowers. Other plants, like the cholla (best described as looking like a cactus sprouting hair) collaborate to accent the desert panorama with vivid colors and fascinating shapes.

The animal life in these desert lands is no less diverse. Large animals, like buckhorn sheep and bobcats are occasionally spotted on this region's rugged mountain slopes; while lower elevations are host to a potpourri of smaller creatures including jackrabbits, squirrels, foxes, and sidewinders.

You'll also share these desert rangelands with an assortment of campers and off-road vehicles. This area draws not only the motoring enthusiast, but also a good number of hikers and nature types. All seem to get along fairly well, although a few complaints are usually voiced concerning the noise from the vehicles crisscrossing the desert floor.

During mild weather months, this area is dotted with trailers and campers. Most set shy of the road, staking out a patch of sandy landscape; folding chairs and beer coolers their essential props. Often parked just a few feet away are several all-terrain vehicles (ATV's), ready for a quick getaway should the mood arise.

For those interested in taking one of these fun vehicles out for some desert antics, ATV's are available for rent by the hour or day near Octillo Wells. Fortunately for us asphalt lovers, most off-roaders stay *off road*, though staying alert for stray ATV's and rat bikes screaming across your path should rank high on your list of "do's".

You'll complete your trip at the junction of Highway 86—a spot that easily qualifies for the label of "middle of nowhere". Those with a sense of culinary adventure can take a trip south on Highway 86 to seek out this region's most infamous delicacy: the date milkshake. Several large stands supply the wayward traveler with more date products than you every thought possible. (Whoever thought that from a palm tree would come such significant and indespensible products as date toothpaste?)

Highway 78's asphalt has received plenty of touch-up work, and overall this roadway is in good shape. You'll notice a slight decline in the quality of pavement as you cross from Imperial County into San Diego County, but the last time through, I found little to be concerned about, whether your vehicle uses two or four wheels.

If you're thinking of tackling this road in the summer, be alert to the perils of desert traveling. As I mentioned, it gets extremely hot during the long summer days, making it essential that you carry plenty of water. People die out here in a matter of hours when they are exposed to high temperatures and lack liquids.

Mechanical breakdowns can also be a frightening experience in this desolate area. With few repair facilities along this highway, it's important that your vehicle be well-maintained—especially its cooling system. If you do experience problems, stay on the road.

Highway 78 is a fine road. The twisty, mountainous course in the first half gives way to miles of high speed straights. Lightly patrolled and in good condition, this highway also leads those with a sense of adventure to other roads. You'll find that most small roads running off of Highway 78 with an "S" designation lead to spirited driving and riding. I particularly recommend S1 and S22 for those seeking byways that provide a more intimate look at this dramatic region of the Golden State.

Highway 79 and Japatul Rd

Direction: North.
Distance: About 95 miles.
Driving time: From two to four hours.
Congestion: Light to medium.
Road condition: Good.
Patrol: Medium.

I'm convinced that a *good* two-laner has embedded deep within its curves and twists a personality. Sometimes playful, occasionally cantankerous, but always entertaining and engaging as it romps about the countryside. Highway 79 and Japatul Road certainly fit that description, often reminding me of two kids left alone in the backyard with a water hose, up to no good, but sure to leave the house standing.

These two twins are at once fun and irreverent; having little to do with getting you from the infamous points of A and B. These friendly threads of asphalt lead the enthusiast down the road to good times.

Calling on a broad range of road that provides the driving and riding enthusiast with an exhilarating and challenging drive, all by itself, little Japatul Road easily covers every demand you could list for a fantastic *driving* road. This little known back trail is one of the best. And by combining it with Highway 79, the traveler has plenty to see, do, and drive—all in less than a 100 miles.

This duo displays a varied collection of scenery that ranges from semi-desert to cool mountain forests. Waiting along the way are plenty of inviting turnouts urging you to pause to enjoy the sights. And the century-old town of Julian lies like a welcomed oasis, providing a wonderful respite from the rigors of traveling.

Our trip begins approximately 30 miles east of San Diego. Take Interstate 8 east from San Diego and exit at Tavern Road. By the time you exit the Interstate, you'll have climbed over 1,700 feet in elevation. Turn right at the exit and you'll be on Tavern Road, in the community of Alpine. You'll spend about five minutes coasting through the outskirts of this small town. The drive out is neither exciting or special, just the best way to get to Japatul Road.

After about three miles, Tavern Road ends in a dogleg to the left, and with a minimum of fuss, you're on Japatul Road. Don't make the mistake of missing the Tavern Road exit off of Interstate 8 and instead take the Japatul Road exit a few miles east. If you do, you'll end up at the end of Japatul Road.

Japatul Road is an exciting squiggle of a road that's well known to the locals. If it was long enough, it would be in this guide on its own merit. But since Japatul Road conveniently joins with Highway 79 at the junction of Interstate 8, I've combined the two roads into one summary.

Japatul Road is a wonderful piece of pavement. In less than 14 miles, it serves up an impressive array of curves and twists as it winds through Cleveland National Park. The first half darts in a southeasterly direction, turning into Japatul Valley Road before heading northeast on the second half.

This back road holds little in the way of hairpin, corkscrew contortions. Scooting along, you'll realize that much of it is easily managed—when driven with just a smidgen of restraint. Yes, your reflexes will still get a good workout, but this trail is laid out so the demanding bits are well dispersed. This road's scorecard is pencilled in with a nifty blend of short straights and enough curling lefts and rights to offer the enthusiast a spirited excursion.

On the weekends, traffic is usually light on Japatul Road. It's a bit more hectic on the weekdays with folks coming to and from work and school. Most homes sit just off the highway, reached by long driveways—making it mandatory that you keep alert for vehicles pulling onto the road.

Japatul Road climbs a good 1,500 feet, though little of it gives the impression of traveling up a sharp incline. For the most part, it's a smooth reach through the mountain peaks and folds of Cleveland National Park. But frankly, I often find the pleasant scenery taking a back seat to the numerous fun driving and riding happenings on Japatul Road.

Japatul Road hands the baton to our main road, Highway 79, at the junction of Interstate 8. (As usual, I'll continue giving you mileage from our starting point in Alpine.) Highway 79 continues the upward trend that started in San Diego. Heading in a northwesterly direction from I-8, the first few miles pay out dividends in tighter, more mountainous driving. The scenery improves too, as you begin driving through forests of lofty oak and pine. Around the 20 mile mark, the road gets narrow in spots and with trees often just inches from the pavement, you'll sometimes find yourself wishing you had a bit more room to maneuver in.

At about the 22 mile mark, you'll enter Samagatuma Valley, where the forests and mountains move away from the road. Driving through scenic valleys and meadows, Highway 79 provides a brief rest from the upward climb you've been making. Tempting the traveler who likes to make frequent stops, this valley holds several large paved turnoffs, rare for a two-lane country road.

Continuing on Highway 79, you'll soon cross the southern border of Cuyamaca Rancho State Park. Leaving Samagatuma Valley means taking on a tight course that again spirals upward. Flanked by trees draped over the roadway, you'll find this a tranquil respite, making it one of the prettiest stretches of Highway 79.

The highway leading up to Lake Cuyamaca is a most agreeable path loaded with fun, challenging bits of pavement. At about the 28 mile mark, you'll glimpse Lake Cuyamaca for the first time. For three miles, Highway 79 follows the contours of this small mountain lake, working the shore in a semi-circle. This serene body of water offers plenty of pleasant views, though with numerous picnic spots and turnoffs dotting its shores, it can get congested. Traffic normally clears considerably upon leaving the lake area.

The six miles between the north end of Lake Cuyamaca and the town of Julian matches a good variety of road with plenty of agreeable scenery. Leading to Julian, the lay of the roadway alternates between moderately tight curves and reasonably straight, well behaved pavement. As the trail once again cuts upward, you'll pass beautiful meadows filled with grazing cattle followed by dense evergreen forests. It's here that you'll begin to appreciate what is certainly one of this byway's main assets: frequent changes in scenery.

Julian, about 40 miles into our trek, is the most engaging community you'll encounter along Highway 79. A gold strike back in 1869 turned this quaint place into a boom town. Once the party ended, Julian turned more to agriculture, and somehow over the years, managed to keep the clutter of commercial development to a minimum. Surrounded by orchards of apple, pear, and peach, tasty homemade pies and jams are for sale everywhere in this homey mountain community. With plenty of quaint little restaurants, this is an ideal place for those with an appetite.

Julian's Main Street is marked by numerous old fashioned false-front buildings. The Julian Hotel is an excellent example of the architectural style that gives this town its unique personality. Creaking wood sidewalks add to the character of this historic community, making Julian an enchanting place to spend an hour or a day.

Leaving Julian, Highway 79 unfurls in an effortless manner, coursing west through rolling foothills. Here, the road consists of mostly mild-mannered curves connected to straights that usually run less than a half mile in length. You'll be driving in a lightly populated rural area that plays host to attractive farms and ranches. The six miles from Julian to Santa Ysabel can get tight in one or two spots, but what really gives this brief run its sense of adventure is a drop in elevation of over 1,200 feet.

With a right turn, you'll leave Santa Ysabel and head north on a long straight pieced together with a few leisurely curves to the right. Most driving enthusiasts will probably increase their speed on this stretch, but be careful. On the remainder of Highway 79, the CHP keeps a much higher profile, giving the last 50 miles a rating of medium in the level of patrol catagory. You'll also see Border Patrol vehicles along this second half. But don't worry about them—unless you've got a dozen illegal aliens roped to the roof of your vehicle.

The 15 miles between Santa Ysabel and Warner Springs consists of unruffled straights and easy low-g sweepers. The elevation remains fairly constant; the few hills you encounter now add to the fun—not the elevation—of your drive. With traffic often light, many enthusiasts will find it tempting to up their speed. The pavement is in good condition—further encouraging a quicker pace. And the scenery is most attractive, with oak trees arranged in a willy-nilly fashion upon the surrounding mountains and foothills.

Another fine stretch of Highway 79 is the first few miles past the junction of Highway 76. Lake Henshaw will be on your left and pretty Mantagual Valley to your right. With cattle grazing against this colorful landscape, the road to Warner Springs scores high marks in the scenery department. By this time, Cleveland National Forest has begun to introduce itself, taking form in the shape of a long mountain range in front of you. At Warner Springs you'll make contact by skirting along the base of this rocky group in a westerly direction.

Leaving Warner Springs, Highway 79 meanders along with hilly curves and bends that offer just the right amount of cut to keep this outing interesting. Near Sunshine Summit, be on the lookout for the giant elephant fronting a trailer park. The sight of this thing (hey, this elephant is *BIG*) always makes me smile. Whoever thought this up certainly has a sense of humor. (Boy, I sure hope this thing was meant to be funny.)

One of the last good straights on Highway 79 is between the small communities of Dodge Valley and Oak Grove. Oak Grove, at about the 70 mile mark, is another of the many delightful sights scattered along the length of Highway 79. By the time you reach this point, you'll begin to notice subtle changes in the landscape. Moving towards Aguanga (about 5 miles down the road from Oak Grove), the terrain turns increasingly arid and desert-like; the mountains add to the geological confusion by frequently swinging to and fro near the road.

From Radac on, travel will be in a westerly direction with the Aqua Tibia Mountains keeping you company off to your left. This is a fine stretch of road made better by the way the hills influence the pavement's course. Past the tiny town of Radac, you'll notice that most straights are marked with two solid yellow lines, indicating that passing is not allowed. They've had problems with drivers trying to get ahead of the crowd on this stretch—with occasionally disasterous results. Use all the caution and good judgement you can muster here. A lot of the straights *really* are a tad too short for passing.

The last five miles of this trip have become increasingly developed. You'll pick up traffic at several junctions as you move towards a meeting with Interstate 15. The road smooths out, easing you onto the day's longest straight as you come out of a sweeping left turn. Running like an arrow through Pauba Valley, our trip finishes at I-15, about 95 miles from our start.

If you're hungry or thirsty, I suggest you head into Temecula, less than a mile away. It's an attractive little town that has become a new "wine country". To reach it, just go under the I-15 overpass and turn right at the first street you encounter.

The road surface on Highway 79 is in consistently good condition. Even Japatul Road is fine, with just a few lumpy patches here and there to keep you honest. I wish I could say all of Highway 79 is lightly patrolled, but as I mentioned, the CHP can get a bit thick on this road's second half.

The back country of San Diego County is an interesting part of California. It offers tourists and locals plenty of good clean fun. Abundant opportunities exist to learn more about California and its fascinating history. From old gold mines near Julian, to this state's newest wine country around Temecula, Highway 79 has something for everyone.

Highway 94

Direction: East.
Distance: About 60 miles.
Driving time: From two to three hours.
Congestion: Medium first half, light second half.
Road condition: Slightly bumpy to excellent.
Patrol: Light.

Having been raised in San Diego, I grew up with this road. The first of many trips along Highway 94 took place when I was seven years old. My folks were playing Good Samaritans by taking some of our motorless Mexican friends to their annual family reunion in Tecate, Mexico. I was in the back seat of our Ford Country Squire with two fat Mexican ladies who seemed to spend most of their time attempting to adjust their newly acquired girdles. Not knowing what a girdle was at that tender age, I figured that by the looks of these two, it was something that made you sweat, itch, and generally feel bad—sort of like measles. And, because these two were *still* so fat, it never occurred to me that it might be a device used to make one look slimmer.

Fortunately, I also have plenty of pleasant thoughts as I reflect back on my first outing along this fine roadway. It was one of those marvelous Southern California winter days, the kind where the sun plays tag with the clouds, unable to decide if it should stay and do its task of warming, or be mischievous and tuck itself behind consenting clouds. As we continued inland, the clouds finally departed for good, leaving us to travel beneath a crystalline sky. And even as a small tike, I loved how this highway carved its way through the wrinkled terrain.

Highway 94, the southernmost road in this book, courses through a part of California where bad weather and heavy traffic often compete for least likely occurrence. But it doesn't pass through the type of California landscapes one finds splashed upon the pages of picturesque travel books. (Highway 79, starting about 35 miles east of San Diego, has much better scenery.) There's no lush national forest drawing the traveler to this road; nor is there much in the way of fancy lodgings or restaurants.

But there are many pleasures to traveling on a road that reflects little of today's cosmopolitan ways. You'll notice that people along this road talk a lot slower than you and me. And their conversations *sound* different than those of city folks.

It's as if terrorism, plane crashes, the always impending wars—all effect people in the little towns differently. Like well-insulated conduit, they go about their business in a way that teaches the observant traveler that the world holds more than what we read in *People* magazine or what the talking heads on TV tell us. Like one farmer told me, a summer filled with bushels of sweet, juicy peaches is an important thing around his place.

You'll find Highway 94 streaking out of San Diego in an easterly direction. You can reach it from both Interstates 5 and 805. The initial westernmost stretch of Highway 94 is actually a freeway so it's not included in this guide. Instead, I begin this summary at a three-way junction called Jamacha Junction, about 12 miles from downtown San Diego.

From this starting point, you'll probably share Highway 94 with a moderate amount of traffic as you first head south, then east, towards the town of Jamul. This is a rural area, with only a few homes and shops dotting the road the first five miles. The gentle nature of this highway is reflected in the initial miles as it rolls along as an easy touring two-laner. The elevation rises about 500 feet on the ten or so miles to Jamul. Traffic will thin out as you continue east, though it's unlikely that you'll lose everyone before Jamul. Luckily, you'll find several pressure relieving straights where you'll be able to pass any traffic lingering in front of you.

The mountains that line the first 20 miles of Highway 94 present themselves in an odd, disorderly fashion. Some are draped in chaparral and sagebrush, while the ones next door might combine rock and vegetation on their flanks, and the rest are just heaps of rock. It looks as if whoever made all the earth's mountains used these rocky pinnacles for practice.

Most enthusiasts don't instantly fall in love with Highway 94 as this trail's early miles seem like anything but great road. But upon leaving Jamul, Highway 94 begins a subtle barter, trading postcard scenery for better motoring action on a ten mile stretch that comprises the 10-20 mile leg of our journey. It now begins to crease through the mountains using a more interesting assortment of bends, twists, and rises. The road is no longer for the shy or easily intimidated, yet neither is this passage one that deals in extremes.

Between the towns of Dulzura and Potrero is a distance of about 12 miles. Upon reaching Potrero you'll have covered about 26 miles since our start at Jamacha Junction. The road now mixes steady climbs using fast curves hung along the shoulders of mountain after mountain. Nearing Potrero, Highway 94 gets downright cantankerous as its path narrows, squeezing and twisting its way forward through this rocky terrain.

Guardrails are for the most part nonexistent through the mountainous portions of this highway. And that's a shame as it's the mountains that give this fun two-laner its encouragement. The safest approach to this highway is generally heading east, the direction used for this book. If you take Highway 94 in the reverse direction, heading back towards San Diego, use care since you'll often be on the cliff side of the road—your wheels spinning just a few feet from steep drops.

If traveling Highway 94 has any other drawback, it's that traffic can be a bit on the heavy side along the first half. Luckily, you'll lose most, if not all of the accompanying traffic at the junction of Highways 94 and 188. Highway 188 is the turnoff for Mexico and the border town of Tecate. Those seeking a quick side trip to Mexico (though this hard working industrial town is not exactly Mexico at its finest) will have less than two miles to travel before reaching the border. Highway 94, especially in its middle miles, often plays tag with the Mexican border, bringing you within a half mile of our southern neighbors at several points. In fact, many of the mountains lying to your right—especially along the middle portion of this road—are within Mexico.

The eleven miles of road on the Potrero-Campo leg is excellent. It's full of tight twists and curves on smooth, well-laid asphalt. Plenty of elevation changes guarantee that this course will produce some exciting maneuvers. Using fast curves slanted on excellent banking, your confidence level will soar as you surge along mile after mile.

This is where Highway 94 gets down to serious business. And with traffic thinning out by Potrero, you can finally add the word secluded to this road's description. Unfortunately, the scenery gets a bit boring at times, replaying the rock-and-chaparral scene a few too many miles for my taste.

Entering Campo is by way of a long valley, much of it used for grazing. But don't let the brief leveling of the road lull you into thinking this roadway is relegated all of its heart-thumping passages to the rearview mirror. After a long straight, Highway 94 gets right back to its tricks. Lots of tight curves and esses over up-and-down hills give the mountain course between Campo and the town of Boulevard high marks in the fun-to-drive department.

I should also mention that Highway 94's road surface is in reasonably good shape for most of its length. Many of the middle miles have been resurfaced recently, making travel a smooth and easy task. After leaving the tiny town of Boulevard you'll lose some of that smoothness as the surface has received less attention here. The one exception is a brief stretch where you'll trade asphalt for concrete— a rarity on back roads.

The final miles of Highway 94, running from Boulevard to the junction of Interstate 8, are a pleasure to drive. Again, it's lightly traveled, but now wide sweepers replace the previous coiling path, allowing the enthusiast to relax a bit. Little among these final miles could create difficulties for the deft driver and rider. Actually, several arrow-like straights are of sufficient length to encourage a visit to the higher numbers printed on your speedometer.

Jacumba is the last town we'll see on Highway 94. There you'll find an agreeable general store stocking everything from cowboy hats to used paperbacks. There's often a crowd of locals out front, and the management has thoughtfully provided a few chairs, encouraging this as a meeting spot.

The scenery on the final minutes of this highway is strangely beautiful. Many of the mountains are strewn with boulders of all shapes and sizes, as if they were made by piling thousands of smaller rocks on each other until someone said, "Enough," and moved on to the next spot. By dominating the landscape, these towering mounds give the terrain a fragile, uneasy posture, looking like they could unravel at the slightest jiggle.

Anyone traveling on Highway 94 will see the brown and white vehicles of the Border Patrol. Working diligently to stem the endless tide of people illegally crossing the border, these folks fight a losing battle. It's hard to be optimistic with so few men and so many hills, gullies, and outlets. Don't worry about getting a traffic violation from the Border Patrol as that's not their job. Traffic enforcement on Highway 94 is handled mainly by the CHP with an assist from the local authorities.

I sleep better at night knowing that a road like Highway 94 exists. Since there's little draw along this road, it's rural nature is safe for now, and there's surely comfort in that. And even though the landscape may get a bit tedious at times, I think you'll find its desolation attractive.

In the driving and riding department, Highway 94 delivers. This road doesn't know how to tease. By providing miles of adventurous pavement that's sure to please the driving and riding enthusiast, its place in this book is assured for a long time to come.

Highway 243

Direction: South.
Distance: 28 miles.
Driving time: About one hour.
Congestion: Light to medium.
Road condition: Good.
Patrol: Light.

Highway 243 is a mountain road that runs helter-skelter through the peaks and forests of the San Jacinto Mountains. These heavily wooded mountains, hiding above the high desert of Southern California, offer a cool summer retreat from the hot valleys that lie at the foot of these mountains. Highway 243 is built along a good range of terrain with spectacular vistas all along its winding path. Taking less than an hour to traverse, it offers a quick fix for those in need of putting a few hard and fast miles on the speedometer.

Highway 243 begins in the high desert community of Banning, about 30 miles east of Riverside. You can bypass most of Banning by taking the Highway 243 exit off of Interstate 10. By doing that, you'll spend but a minute driving through a semi-rural area before reaching our target road.

The first mile of Highway 243 is a quiet straight that takes aim at the rocky pinnacles filling the horizon before you. Soon after, a sharp upward left will whisk you off of the desert floor towards a loftier road. Heading upwards, Highway 243 sports a fairly steep grade, making high speeds more difficult to come by. And that's fine since the first five miles contain a wealth of tight, tricky curves. It's amazing how quickly you rise off of the desert floor. And the effect it has on the scenery is no less impressive. Though the initial view of Banning is nondescript, a rise in height brings with it a different perspective—showing a quilt-like layout—the new-found distance softening many of the blemishes of this imperfect community.

The first six miles give you a fantastic road in good condition and flanked by great scenery. You'll see a few of the tighter turns posted with curve speed signs, but for the most part, you'll be on your own. Guardrails are limited to the tighter curves on this first stretch—leaving the straights and sweepers unbroached by retaining devices. Those of you who take this road aggressively will find a lot of pleasure in second and third gear. If you prefer a more leisurely pace, much of this section can be taken in fourth—if your vehicle's gearing isn't too tall. The road surface is in fine condition and both the center and shoulder lines have recently been repainted.

By the seven mile mark, you'll notice that our course takes a less coiled path. Highway 243 started by slashing along the shoulders of mountains, but now it takes you deep inside those mountains, into its rocky folds, away from the breathtaking vistas that were such a beautiful part of the first section. The road remains entertaining, with quick little bursts the order of the day as you find scant relief from the continuing climb. Around eight miles out, you'll cross the boundary of the San Bernardino National Forest—bringing with it mountains covered in pine, bestowing the rocky slopes with a lovely hue of green.

Around 11 miles out you'll pass the 5,000 foot mark in elevation. Along with a change in scenery from desert to mountain forest, you'll also find the temperature getting cooler at the higher elevations—even downright cold if it's anytime besides summer. And, as if in apology for losing the views back towards the north, Highway 243 begins to frame in big panoramas the spectacular land of forests and mountains that lie to the south and west of you. Equally dramatic views are spread throughout the remainder of Highway 243, and with plenty of scenic overlooks and turnoffs, it's easy to stop for picture taking and sightseeing.

At the half way point—around the Lake Fulmor turnoff—Highway 243 becomes better behaved. Though certainly not straight enough to be considered an easy tour, these middle miles contain a few straights connected to more sweepers than we've seen yet on Highway 243. A brief respite from potential boredom is offered on a quick run along a nifty batch of esses at around the 18 mile mark. But watch out, this roadway can be relentless in the way it lays down decreasing radius curves when you least expect them, especially when leaving a straight and setting up for the next curve in the road.

The landscape in the 11-20 mile leg consists mainly of mountains covered in pine forests. Great heaps of granite, many chunks bigger than a car, stand sentinel along the road, helping to break up the palette of greens that the forest provides.

The first mountain community you come upon is Alandale. If traffic is light, you'll probably miss this town. Pine Cove and Idyllwild, both bigger and just a few minutes up the road, offer plenty of restaurants and lodging to the traveler. None of the towns on Highway 243 offer the quaintness or historical interest of California towns like Julian or Sonora. But both Pine Cove and Idyllwild do seem like pleasant enough places. And, like any road that handles all of the comings and goings of a community, the two and a half mile stretch of road between Pine Cove and Idyllwild can get a bit congested. With limited speeds (25-30 mph range) enforced, the pace can be slow at times.

The last three miles, from the outskirts of Idyllwild to where Highway 243 ends at Mountain Center, is a pleasant surprise for the enthusiast. If you can shake the traffic, you'll have several nice runs on road reminiscent of the fantastic chunk that opened your drive on Highway 243—with one exception: the direction is down instead of up. Also, the twists seem better marked with curve speed advisory information than on the first half of our trip. And since your descent can be quite steep after leaving Pine Cove, you should plan on reducing your speed accordingly, especially on the curves. Lying in wait are several wide sweepers that take so long to complete that the emblem on your steering wheel begins to look natural sideways.

Some of the prettiest stretches of Highway 243 are between Pine Cove and Idyllwild. In several places the pines are high enough to shade the road completely, making you feel like you're in an enchanted forest. Other miles will find the foliage sparser. All provide an ever changing portrait of the layers of mountains that, at times, seem to run off in all directions.

You'll finish up at the junction of Highway 74. There you'll find a small restaurant that was serving up a fairly decent breakfast and even better Mexican food the last time I was there. At first glance, this road might seem like it's out in the middle of nowhere, but I use it to get from Los Angeles to the Palm Springs resort area. By turning left at Highway 74 (also in this guide), you'll be just 50 miles from Palm Springs. The alternate route, Interstate 10, pales in comparison to these two fine roads.

In summary, Highway 243 has several things going for it. First, traffic is extremely light on much of this road. Second, the asphalt is in great condition, especially on the two blissful sections comprising the start and finish of out trek. The only stretch of Highway 243 that's susceptible to rock slides (clearly marked) is in the early going. Of course, I'd be amiss if I didn't mention that I rarely see this road patrolled. Unfortunately, during winter, Mother Nature can bring plenty of snow to this highway—especially at the higher elevations—effectively making this a warm weather passage only.

I love driving mountain roads. The good ones offer the enthusiast plenty of variety by the way they sculpt their way through the rock. The best roads also provide scenic relief and enough places to pull over whenever the urge strikes. And, last but not least, these rocky highways are not so popular that you feel like you're getting in line when you first arrive on the road. Highway 243 passes in all categories. And even though it's not quite up to the sporting nature of Angeles Crest Highway or Angeles Forest Highway, it still provides plenty of fun for the enthusiast lucky enough to unlock its secrets.

CHAPTER 4

BEST
ROADS
OF
CENTRAL
CALIFORNIA

Highway 1 (near Lompoc)

Direction: North.
Distance: About 65 miles.
Driving time: From two to three hours.
Congestion: Light.
Road condition: Very good.
Patrol: Light to medium. Heavy in Lompoc.

This varied stretch of Highway 1 is unknown to many. Yet it packs plenty of fantastic driving into a very short distance. This impressive road offers everything from wide open cruising to a sensational mountain course where skilled drivers and riders will find plenty of sport. Toss in great scenery and you have the makings of one of California's best roadways.

Our starting point for this section of Highway 1 is reached by an exit off of Highway 1. It's the first exit for Vandenberg Air Force Base—about two and a half miles north of where Highway 101 turns inland after traveling along the picturesque California shoreline. Those coming from the Santa Barbara area have about a half hour drive.

The first leg of our trip on Highway 1—running from Highway 101 to the junction of Highway 246—is 18 miles of fine two-lane. As you exit Highway 101, you'll have an additional passing lane to quickly put accompanying traffic in your rearview mirror. Initially, you'll be driving through rolling hills that are home for little more than a few private ranches. This stretch has received extensive resurfacing, leaving the asphalt in excellent condition.

The first 18 miles of this road seem to encourage the loosening of the throttle as it speeds through the valleys caught between the Santa Ynez Mountains on wide, smooth sweepers. Though slightly hilly at times, there are few surprises in the first ten miles. Up to this point, the mountains have kept their distance. But they'll close in at about the ten mile mark. Mother Nature forces the road to become more adventurous as Highway 1 aggressively pursues the contours of the land. Staying tightly curled for about a mile, Highway 1 again loosens up at about the 11 mile mark.

Less than 14 miles into our jaunt, you'll encounter the White Hills and that means tighter, more curvaceous road for a moment.

Nothing wicked, just a few playful esses to keep your spirits up. Consider it rehearsal for what lies north of Lompoc. The first 18 miles comes to a close at the stop sign where Highways 1 and 246 meet. A left turn keeps you on Highway 1, heading towards Lompoc.

Our path now courses through the best and worst that Lompoc has to offer (though many might not be able to tell the difference). If relieving hunger is a priority, then this town can fit the bill. For those who feel at home in the fast-food jungles, Lompoc will look like Mecca. It might be a good time to gas up, too. You'll need to make a couple of turns to navigate through Lompoc, but all are clearly posted. Unfortunately, the traffic lights in Lompoc seem to be timed for something other than motorized vehicles.

As you leave Lompoc you'll encounter moderate to heavy traffic, but most of it will make the left turn for Vandenberg Air Force Base. This turnoff is located on the northern outskirts of Lompoc, about a mile past the sign announcing the end of the 45 mph speed limit. From there, Highway 1 becomes a reasonably straight, though hilly roadway.

Some of these hills are quite pronounced, and capable of giving you that queasy feeling you'd get as a kid when your dad would drive quickly up and down a hill—leaving your stomach back a ways. If your Dad was anything like mine, then you probably caught a brief glimpse of his mischievous grin in the rearview mirror. There he was, beaming with smug satisfaction, knowing that he had just committed perfectly legal revenge on you for not cleaning your room, or throwing up on your little sister at her birthday party, or any number of travesties you had recently performed in your feeble attempts at being a well behaved child.

And it was at the bottom of a hill just like these on Highway 1, that, as a small tike, I first learned that liquids could mysteriously go up your nose—rather than into one's stomach. As the Coke dripped out of my nose, I felt disbelief; thinking that I must have broken some bone or other important component in my face that would allow this oddity to happen.

As tears welled up in my eyes from the burning of my sinuses, I readied myself for what now felt like certain death. As I prepared to say my final goodbyes, suddenly—and without warning—my mom began to spank me from the front seat for drooling on myself and my new shirt. During the spanking, it began to dawn on me that I probably would live through all of this. Though after my punishment, the intense pain emanating from my bottom made me wonder if death by drooling might have been the better way to go.

Anyway, keep an eye out for these hills on Highway 1, as a lot of them are blind, making aggressive driving a foolish idea. As you near the end of the hills, Highway 1 brings a few interesting off-camber twists to the table, so keep alert.

At about the 24 mile mark you'll become aware of a small mountain lying ahead. You're now closing in one one of the best pieces of mountain driving in California. It's two lanes—and narrow ones at that. Climbing this mountain path through the Purisima Hills is a thorough test of machines and reflexes.

My friends and I have nicknamed this little passage the Purisima Pass. Foolish, aggressive drivers will be humbled by this road. But skilled drivers will enjoy this road immensely. Drivers with questionable abilities would do best to take this road slow and easy the first few times. And stupid, lead-footed types will simply see this road as an endless series of precipitous cliffs. This, my friends, is a passage that requires finesse.

Now for a few details. The Purisima Pass begins with a sharp, upward left-handed turn posted at 20 mph. Climbing quickly, you'll be greeted by a constant barrage of lefts, rights, and every variation of up, down, and around that you ever thought existed. Carved through one tough mountain, this part of Highway 1 quickly defines the limits of your driving ability. Though this mountain jaunt lasts just over two miles, you'll swear it's longer.

Some of you might think that I'm making a big deal over such a short stretch of road. But to me, this inspiring passage elicits the same reponse as a good amusement park ride: though only lasting a couple of minutes, when it's over, all you can think about is getting back in line for another go-around. For those who love endless curves and twists, a visit to this stretch of Highway 1 should be near the top of your list. And if you feel the need to stop and catch your breath, there are ample turnouts (many with nice views) on this mountain road.

After that you might think it gets easy, right? Wrong. Next comes the esses of the San Antonio Valley. These little jewels are the perfect compliment to the mountain driving you've just finished. After a mile or so, these esses drop you onto the valley floor. A long straight, tucked between fields, ends this section unceremoniously at a lone stop sign.

I'm always amazed at the amount of fantastic driving packed into these five miles. And if that wasn't enough, let me mention two other advantages: this section is lightly traveled and the pavement on this pass and the adjoining twisting road is in good condition. You'll see a rock or two on the mountainous stretch, but normally there are few road hazards to maneuver around.

After turning left at the stop sign, the next section of Highway 1 heads north—straight as an arrow. You'll have two lanes on your side of the road. And even though it's on a slight incline, I've seen speeds of well over 100 mph on the stretch between San Antonio Road and the overpass that marks the junction of country road S20. With a little over two miles to stretch it out, the pavement underneath is in terrific shape, furthering the urge to throttle down. After a quick two miles, traffic will join you from your right—as S20 signs up with Highway 1—making it difficult to safely continue any sort of high speed run.

When you come to a fork on Highway 1, take the left one, towards Guadalupe. It's here that your brief interlude with a divided highway ends. Ahead lies 10 miles of rural farm road that, when not laden with farm vehicles, is geared for speed. About three and a half miles after leaving the four-lane behind, you'll come to an intersection that halts traffic with a four-way stop sign. This is the junction of Black Road and Highway 1.

After passing Black Road, you'll find seven miles of flat, almost straight roadway slicing through fertile farmlands. Heading northwest on this often deserted road, many drivers find it impossible to keep their speed down. You'll traverse a rural area that offers little in the way of diversions or traffic (especially on the weekends) and patrol is usually light.

Upon passing Brown Road, traffic can get heavy, usually requiring a major reduction in speed. Plan on driving behind at least one large, smoke-belching truck as it carts produce away from the fields that dot this region. The ride into Guadalupe is uneventful except for a pretty cemetery on your left, as you enter town.

Guadalupe, home for the Mexican folks that live and work in this area, is as honest as they come. No glitzy shopping malls or fancy boutiques here. Many of the town's signs and placards along the simple main street are in Spanish, reflecting the language of the people this town diligently serves. It's not a pretty place, but in many ways it accurately reflects the haunting, yet always hopeful outlook of the hard working itinerate farm workers who inhabit this area.

Upon leaving Guadalupe, you're likely to once again share the road with produce trucks and farm vehicles. During certain times of the year, a lot of dust gets kicked up by the wind from the numerous support trucks and tractors working the fields. Nothing serious, but it can cut visibility and make your eyes water a bit.

As the road rises up off the valley floor, you'll discover several groves of fragrant eucalyptus trees. Leaving the straights back in the valley, you'll have a good range of turns, sometimes sharp, but with warning speeds posted. There are a good many hills—a few blind—so use caution when coming up over any rise. You'll have a nice combination of hilly straights leading into fiesty curves that'll require a high level of intimacy with the brake pedal if you are to safely traverse the fastest corners.

Confrontations with man are no less comforting in the later miles of Highway 1. The big Union Oil plant is hard to miss, and small beatup trailers sitting in weed-clogged lots will make you feel lucky to live where you do. This is not a road festooned with bright lights and tourist attractions.

About 10 miles out of Guadalupe you have one final, fun dash to sea level as you come over a rise overlooking the beautiful and compact Cienaga Valley. For a brief moment you'll be high enough to enjoy the quilt-like layout of this pretty little valley. With alternating squares of green crops and brown unplanted fields, it's a sight city folks rarely see.

Nearing the end of our trek, the drive through Oceano is boring and uneventful. Look to the left and you'll be able to catch glimpses of sand dunes that have helped give dune buggies and all-terrain vehicles such a fun reputation. You'll finish up at the beach town of Pismo Beach. Though no Malibu, it's not as ugly as Oceano. If the weather is good—or it's summertime—you'll find a lot of tourists, children, traffic, and police in and around Pismo Beach.

A final sweeping right turn through Pismo Beach lands you at the junction of Highway 101—the end of our trek on Highway 1. For those weary travelers needing gas or a bathroom, there's a Mobil station conveniently sitting to your right. Highway 1 starts up again about 12 miles north of Pismo Beach and can be reached via Highway 101, heading north. From there it leads you into lovely Morro Bay and onto the next section of Highway 1 featured in this guide.

Though this stretch of Highway 1 is often overshadowed by the famous link of Highway 1 north of here, this is still easily one of the best roads in California. And no matter what kind of driving environs you lust after, you're sure to be accommodated by this enjoyable road.

Highway 1 (Coast route)

Direction: North.
Distance: About 120 miles.
Driving time: Four to eight hours.
Congestion: Medium to heavy.
Road condition: Average, though rough in spots.
Patrol: Medium.

It was winter 1922. A lone worker, dangling from ropes suspended over a perpendicular cliff, having placed his first explosive charges, reached into his soiled overalls for a tattered handkerchief while waiting to be pulled up to the cliff edge. Wiping his eyes of the sting of volcanic dust that often lingered in the air after each explosion, he found little time to enjoy the spectacle of ocean and mountain that lay around him.

A quarter mile south, near Anderson Creek, new explosions echoed hard against the cliffs, subsiding ever so slowly. Loud, ferocious belts of sound that this farm boy had never heard before today. A violent fury ripping at the bellies of countless mountains. Day in, day out. Transforming rock into highway, foot by foot, stone by stone, Highway 1 was etched into the California coastline.

He was a restless eighteen year-old who migrated in the summer of '22 to California from his home in the peaceful farmlands of Tennessee. Finding employment with the George Pollard Company of Sacramento, his first job was to help build Highway 1, south of Big Sur. He went by the name of Willie Tucker.

He was my great uncle.

Forty years later, while on vacation in Tennessee, I discovered a battered hope chest tucked away in a dark corner of the musty basement of his parent's sprawling farm. Inside, I found the letters he had written to them while working on Highway 1. From those yellowed sheets of paper came these thoughts about sacrificing such majestic land for the sake of a road:

"The work is slow, hard and never endin'." he wrote from a letter dated 9 November 1922, "Yet, everyday we somehow creep a tad north. And not the hardest rock or stone can stop this crew. These mountains that we root up are old and beautiful, feels sorta like somebody's grandpa to me, and it's a cryin' shame to rid the land of 'em."

The letter continued, "I been makin' my crew get down an pray before each one's blown. They think I'm crazy. But I jus' tell 'em, these mountains is like God's first churches—and we'd be smart ta let Him know that we ain't *too* proud of what we been doin'."

My great uncle toiled for three long years, braving often intolerable conditions, before using his hard earned savings to settle in a small seaside hamlet a few miles north of where he labored; certainly far enough away so as not to be within earshot of the explosions he found so painful. It was there in a small colony called Carmel that a view lot, surrounded by cool pine, could be had for several hundred dollars. He stayed for over two decades, before finally returning to his home in Tennessee in the late 1940's.

This is certainly one of those roads whose history is as colorful as the drive itself. Back in 1915, with World War I still echoing in many ears, it was easier to get the initial planning funds for Highway 1 appropriated from the state legislature using the argument that this road was imperative for the defense of the country—not because it would unlock some of California's premier scenery to the newly motoring masses. Finally, in 1919, the state's voters approved an initial $1.5 million (good for about 50 feet of crooked sidewalk these days), with the actual construction beginning just north of San Simeon in 1921.

The building of this scenic section of Highway 1 continued on and off for nearly 20 years, when, at last, in 1937 you could drive from San Simeon to Carmel on paved road. Political maneuvering, bad weather, rugged terrain, difficult working conditions—all played a role in making the building of this road a long and difficult proposition. Construction actually stopped in the mid-1920's before a newly elected governor agreed to help revive the construction program.

During the course of construction, convict labor (many from San Quentin), augmented by a cheap Chinese labor force, performed much of the arduous and dangerous work necessary to build this road. Work gangs, often working with nothing but a pick and shovel, slaved during long 14-hour days to complete this road. Final cost is said to have been just under $10 million!

When I mentioned to people that I was working on a guide to California's best roads, I invariably heard one question time and again: "You mean roads like Highway 1?" From interviews with automobile and motorcycle enthusiasts, it became clear that this stretch of Highway 1 is everyone's favorite. Slicing north along California's jagged coastline, this byway, running from Morro Bay to the Monterey Peninsula, is easily the most famous stretch of highway in California—if not North America.

But even though this twin-laner comes complete with an imposing reputation, it's an immensely likeable road, full of spectacular scenery and miles of friendly pavement. To please the adventurous driver and rider, sections of this road are packed with tight runs along ever present cliffs, whisking you along a road that's often described as having been engineered with a gleeful lunacy. If you plan on doing any recreational driving or riding in California, this is the one road you won't want to miss.

We begin this journey upon Highway 1 in the sea town of Morro Bay. This lovely, grown-up fishing village offers the traveler plenty of options in the lodging and restaurant departments. In addition, the world's best shrimp-cocktail-in-a-styrofoam-cup is found right on the harbor in Morro Bay at a place called Finicky Fish Market No.2 (I have no idea where No. 1 is). For a paltry sum (usually less than three bucks), you get great tasting shrimp smothered in a delicious homemade cocktail sauce.

We often stop next door at Virg's Sportfishing and pick up a couple of cold ones to go along with our shrimp and sourdough bread (also available at Finicky's) and aim for the beach that's less than a minute away. Once there, you can park on a short bluff overlooking Morro Rock and a most pleasant stretch of beach.

Getting started on Highway 1 from Morro Bay is a cinch: go north for about a mile or so on Main Street, keeping an eye out for the clearly marked onramp. Starting life as a modern, elevated four-lane freeway, you'll find Highway 1 continuing its impressive imitation of a streamlined roadway for about seven miles. Initially, the road is made up of wide low-g sweepers and long straights, certainly nothing to press the skilled enthusiast.

There are few bends or twists to complicate your forward progress in the early going. Instead you'll find the scenery stealing the show on these first few miles. To your left lies Morro Bay, where portions of the shoreline remain relatively undeveloped. A few miles further, scenic Estero Bay takes center stage as Highway 1 continues to hold up a bounty of striking scenes.

After seven miles, Highway 1 trims down to two lanes as it continues to run near parallel with the shoreline for several miles. To your right lies the untamed coastal range known as the Santa Lucia Range, a constant companion for the length of this journey.

By the small town of Harmony, the roadway will have swept the traveler up over 1,700 feet. The six miles from Harmony to Cambria bring you safely back to near sea level. Several miles before Harmony you'll also temporarily lose your view of the ocean. It's replaced with attractive terrain shaped into the form of rolling foothills, often thick with herds of grazing cattle.

Cambria, our next seaside town, lies about 20 miles from Morro Bay. Here we swing closer to the dramatic shoreline. I first discovered

Cambria in the early 1960's, when it was still a sleepy little borough. Today it fights to remain true to its early origins as a fine spot to build a vacation or retirement home. Here the pace is slow and the people most friendly. Just the thought of its cool, Alpine-like setting, full of groves of pine overlooking the California coastline, conjures up vivid memories of the rich images that help define this stretch of California coastline.

The ugliest piece of Highway 1 has got to be San Simeon's collection of motels, restaurants, and gift shops that lie just a few minutes north of Cambria. This conglomeration—with its seemingly solitary purpose— provides tourists with a most unattractive place to stay and eat while touring nearby Hearst Castle.

Hearst Castle is easily the most famous man-made attraction along our route. Now a state historic monument, guided tours are the only way you and I can get inside this lavish, palatial home created for publishing mogul, W.R. Hearst. Various tours, each taking about two hours, enable you to see different sections of this grand estate. The turnoff to Hearst Castle is clearly marked. Traffic will lighten considerably beyond this turnoff since many of your fellow motorists have the castle in mind as a final destination.

If the earlier blight of motels and restaurants caused you pain, you can catch a tranquil bit of history by making the left turn marked "W.R. HEARST STATE BEACH". It's less than 30 miles into our journey. Drive down about one half mile and you'll hit Sebastian's. This venerable general store, built in 1873, is a combination deli, gift, and hardware store. Brousing through this well stocked pavilion, you'll be hard pressed to think of something you need that Sebastian's doesn't stock.

Sitting back off of Highway 1, Sebastian's comes complete with a squeaky old wood porch. Entering through a screen door (when was the last time you entered a business through a screen door?), you'll immediately be hit by the old-fashioned sounds and smells of this quiet place. Those longing for a more personal approach to running a business will find solace here.

A restaurant attached to Sebastian's offers reasonably good food (very good breakfasts) and is open from April to October. A few choice outside tables are available for soaking up any good weather you might have the fortune of encountering.

Well, I know that I haven't spent much time covering what the enthusiast can expect while on this section of Highway 1. It's been mainly gentle curves and long straights for the first 30 miles, ideal for enjoying the dazzling scenery. This isn't the kind of pavement that subjects drivers and riders to heartpounding situations—though the magnificent vistas are guaranteed to take your breath away more than once.

60

The motoring experience gets a bit more interesting north of Hearst Castle. The 30 to 40 mile leg offers several runs on narrow, somewhat tight road, though none of the fun chunks of asphalt last longer than a minute or two. You'll also be greeted by a few bends posted with 55 mph curve speeds, implying that you might have been actually going faster than the speed limit (not you!). But overall, most stretches along here are fairly straight and uneventful, again, making it easy to enjoy the incredible scenery along this portion of Highway 1.

Those lucky enough to have clear weather along this scenic route will enjoy the sight of seemingly endless miles of mountainous silhouettes as the rugged shoreline merges into the white-tipped waters of the Pacific. Unfortunately, this region is also well known for its fog and mist. During winter's short days, when the cold wintry winds whip over the cliffs and mountains, sightseeing becomes a blustery experience. Summers are usually a bit more hospitable to the traveler, though the early morning fog and mist can often make it feel like even August has been seized by winter's cold grasp.

Just past the 40 mile mark, you'll see an ominous sign—like some kind of disclaimer—announcing that this road is dangerous during storms (true), and it's not maintained at night (usually true). Acting like the opening credits to a slam-bang, shoot-em-up, adventure movie, you're now in for the best Highway 1 has to offer the serious enthusiast.

Flying high above the expansive ocean, you'll bustle along a narrow two-laner that twitches and turns like a wounded snake looking for one last victim. Switchbacks abound, and few guardrails are present to protect the innocent—easily making this the boldest installment of Highway 1. It's a path cut with fast corners, hung out to dry along the sharp rims of sheer cliffs; the great abyss that seems to lie off of each helps emphasize how important it is to judge each twirl of the road with the utmost accuracy. For as beautiful as this road can be, it can be as equally unforgiving. Exploring this section of highway, a tug-of-war begins to rage; with the great heights and vistas battling for your attention versus wicked pavement that's built to provide the enthusiast with an exhilarating motoring experience.

There are numerous places to pull off along Highway 1, though most are on the opposite (ocean side) of the road, making this an often dangerous move to perform. But what's most difficult about driving this coiling section of Highway 1 is fighting back the impatience you'll have with the numerous slow moving vehicles ahead of you. Those anxious for open road may find themselves, in their urge for freedom, making maneuvers that can be deadly. Here, restraint can be a lifesaving virtue.

These cliff-clinging, serpentine stretches are not in the best of shape. To your right lie perilously crumbling slopes—constantly releasing marbles upon a road that's already short on shoulders and long on blind curves.

61

But the biggest threat to Highway 1 comes from mudslides, which caused one of the longest closures of Highway 1 in 1983. Severe Pacific storms saturated the ground just south of Big Sur so heavily with water that tons of earth came sliding down onto Highway 1 in a thick, syrupy mass of mud. The road remained closed to all through traffic for over a year while crews worked frantically to clear the mire covering this scenic trail.

By the time you reach Gorda, about 55 miles into our journey, the road will have straightened considerably. Oh, you'll still have a few curves and turns, but much of the unruly pavement will be behind you, giving way to straighter, less demanding curves and bends. Plenty of elevation changes along this course make the sights even *more* spectacular with the perspective changing as each shift in height presents a different view of this broken, ragged coastline.

The 60-to-80 mile leg brings with it additional straight road, though Highway 1 continues to please (tease?) by throwing in sets of twistys every now and then. The scenery continues to be unbelievable in sheer breadth and size. Highway 1 rears back and throws the book at you—everything from beautiful bridges suspended over lush green canyons to towering mountains covered in dense forests.

It's near here that you encounter the towering redwood's southernmost toehold. These giants of the forest hug the shoreline of California, progressing north for well over 400 miles. Seeking a recipe of cool mist, fog, and rain, these kings rarely venture inland from the narrow patch of paradise that Mother Nature has so thoughtfully provided for their growth and protection.

Big Sur.

Those two words invoke a myriad of images. It's a place where the toughness of the battered seaside cliffs is equalled by the tenaciousness of its residents. Fiercely independent, the proud people of this area are quick to rally against anything or anyone who could harm the wilderness they call home. Travel through these hinterlands is, at best, done with an uneasy truce with nature.

Big Sur is also a haven for those seeking enlightenment—though often spiritual gratification comes at a lofty price that reflects the exclusivity of the resorts that engage in those activities. Fortunately, the commerce of spirituality is contrasted by Big Sur's anachronous warriors of the 1960's, people who never saw the act of fighting for a cause as a trend, or a stage one goes through while growing up.

Big Sur's geological surroundings are in no less of a conflict. The imposing Santa Lucia Mountains work overtime, protecting Big Sur's backside while playing host to the untamed wilderness of the Los Padres National Forest. The opposite side of Highway 1 reveals the formidable Pacific Ocean; slowly, relentlessly reclaiming a rocky shoreline that once lay below its surface before violent earthquakes and fiery volcanoes pushed the ocean back a crumbling arm's length. With tourism continuing to increase, the area's seemingly eternal battle between the protection and usage of these beautiful lands is unlikely to abate soon.

The final 30 miles of our trip, from Big Sur north to Carmel, offer a potpourri of pavement: a few switchbacks intertwine with short winding stretches, all squeezed between long chunks of smooth, slightly arced highway. On occasion, densely packed layers of pine and redwood shroud this highway—unlike the miles of unprotected shoreline that have preceded us. Though this tunnel-like drive only lasts a few minutes, the towering evergreens make for a refreshing change of pace.

As you close in on Carmel, traffic will increase. But once again, the scenery comes to the rescue. Every curve brims with a rich panorama of mountain, forest, and ocean—harmoniously linked into an awe-inspiring vision of nature. Highway 1 rides atop the final, jutting slivers of rock, giving you plenty of opportunities to stop and photograph many of the sights that have become the "scenic trademarks" of this stretch of California coastline: small pristine beaches, secluded coves tucked between fingers of rock, and white waves by the fistfulls, chiseling away at any rocky outcropping that dares to defy its relentless force.

The last five miles are through the exclusive communities of Carmel Highlands and Carmel. You'll see plenty of beautiful homes and mansions on this final stretch of Highway 1. Your first view of Carmel Bay will be hard to forget, with Cypress trees—those twisted, tortured-looking masses of wood—gracing the ever changing shoreline.

Carmel, our finishing point, continues to find quaintness an increasingly elusive label to hold on to when thousands of tourists jam your streets, fill your limited parking spaces, and buy your goods by the millions of dollars every month. (Monterey, with its dramatic new aquarium and historic, but touristy Cannery Row, lies less than ten minutes north of here and fights a similar, though less publicized battle.)

There are excellent arts and crafts being created in this area. In fact, Carmel began life as an artist's colony. But escalating prices forced all but the richest of artisans to flee to cheaper—though no less beautiful—surroundings, like Big Sur to the south. Many of the stores in Carmel (and Big Sur, too, for that matter) proudly display the work of local artists to an eager-to-buy public. Oh, you'll find plenty of T-shirt type stores, but I think you'll be genuinely impressed by the quality of goods for sale in bustling Carmel.

Even though this road is very popular, much of Highway 1 remains unspoiled. Roads like this aren't built anymore. And it seems the scenic highway, too, has become an increasingly endangered species. Fortunately, it was the fragile beauty of this highway and the surrounding land that motivated legislators to establish the scenic highway program, with Highway 1 the first road to be put under its protective banner.

Alas, this great road can be made miserable by the glut of motor homes and campers that clog this picturesque lane. During the summer, you'll encounter what seems like thousands of rubbernecking tourists—their necks crammed up to the little windows of lumbering tonage—all with that stupid-looking, "me-too" horizontal brown stripe running down the middle.

It's not that I hate campers, it's just I do not understand why the manufacturers of these rolling bomb shelters do not follow the lead of the automotive industry and build them with more power and better handling characteristics. All of the people who drive near and around these monsters would be better for it.

Another word of caution: don't even think of driving this road at night. Sections of it are difficult enough during the day, let alone in the black of night. No fun, no way.

Also, the CHP, from their office in Salinas, employs a decent amount of manpower to patrol this stretch of Highway 1. Weekends can find the patrol a bit on the heavy side, but you'll not find any CHP spotter planes on this roadway, nor have I ever seen radar used.

Overall, I think the views on this excursion are a tad more impressive moving in a southerly direction—especially on the bottom half of Highway 1. This is also the safer route since most of the turnoffs are on your right-hand side as you head south. The views are about equal along the northern half, though northbound drivers definitely have the best views heading into Carmel.

California's flagship road is a driving, visual, and engineering marvel. This fun, winding passage bares to the traveler some of the most beautiful scenery in the world. A ride along Highway 1 almost makes you feel cheated when you think about retreating to your own neck of the woods.

Highway 1's grand reputation is well deserved, I think. And as you near the end of this road, full of memories of this trail's engaging personality, you're likely to find yourself wishing it would go on forever. But that's how a good road works, always leaving you wanting more.

Seventeen Mile Dr (Hwy 17)

Direction: Pick em'.
Distance: 17 big ones.
Driving time: From two hours on up.
Congestion: Unconfirmed rumors of high speed turbo golf carts.
Road condition: Sometimes dangerous due to flying golf balls.
Patrol: Running battle between police and grounds keepers for road supremacy.

Let me say right off, that it would border on the criminal to not include a roadway with its own color brochure in a book on the best roads of Calfornia. (Now *that's* style.) And even though at 17 miles in length it doesn't meet the minimum mileage criteria (25 miles) for this guide, I've included it anyway because it's a fine little drive that's not to be missed if you plan to spend any time on the Monterey Peninsula.

The scenery on 17 Mile Drive is spectacular as it meanders through beautiful Del Monte Forest and the exclusive community of Pebble Beach. It also takes in a fabulous stretch of the rocky Pacific Ocean shoreline complete with barking seals and other great aquatic events. You'll even pass among golf courses charging upwards to a 100 bucks for a chance to lose your dimpled little ball in the most splendid of scenery. And as if that wasn't enough, you'll often be surrounded by palatial mansions so big they could easily qualify as small towns. (Luckily, a potentially devastating fire in the spring of 1987 left nary a mark on the beautiful scenery along this road.)

But, I have to admit that some enthusiasts will only like this road if you agree that constantly getting in and out of your car to gawk at the great views is a part of the motoring experience. Unfortunately, all of the curves and twists of this road come with near terminal traffic and hazards. Hey, what can I say? I'm a sucker for any road with snazzy guard gates and its own ad campaign.

Last time I was there the entrance fee was up to five bucks—a small price to pay for a cruise along 17 miles of paradise.

Highway 33

Direction: North.
Distance: About 55 miles.
Driving time: From two to three hours.
Congestion: Very light.
Road condition: Good, except where noted.
Patrol: Light, except for the first five miles.

I first heard about Highway 33 from my friend, Bobby Hardison. For quite a while, Bobby raced motorcycles, sprint cars, and who knows what else, before a back injury put him into a safer and saner line of work. When I mentioned that I was working on a guide to the best roads of California, he immediately brought up this intriguing, remote highway.

People like Bobby—people who truly love to drive and ride—have been an invaluable source of information for this book. His eloquent recital of this highway's attributes had me itching to get on this road. And now it's become one of my favorites. Bobby and I talk about getting out on Highway 33 and running it like there's no tomorrow (but heh, that's another story, better left for another time...).

If you've read much of this guide, you know that I usually start my narrative at the junction of a major freeway or town. It makes sense when you realize that most of you will be coming from a major freeway or city to get to each road's starting point. But for this road, I suggest you avoid beginning your drive on Highway 33 at the junction of Highway 101.

If you insist on taking Highway 101 to Highway 33, be prepared for five miles of boring, four-lane freeway that runs through a bleak-looking industrial area. The remaining eight miles to the junction of Highway 150 isn't a stretch you'd write home about either, though it's an improvement over the first five miles. This initial stretch passes through the small towns of Casitas Springs and Oak View. You'll often have a 45 mph speed limit to adhere to. And until you get past Highway 150, there's little on Highway 33 that resembles fun road. Another negative is the moderate to heavy traffic.

So, we begin our trek about a mile and a half west of the community of Ojai, at the junction of Highways 33 and 150. If you're

66

coming from the Los Angeles area, I suggest you take Interstate 5 north, to Highway 126 west. That'll lead you to Santa Paula and Highway 150, upon which you'll travel a pleasant 18 miles before finding Highway 33.

As you begin, the drive through the outskirts of Ojai seems to go quickly even though you're limited by a 40 mph speed limit for the first mile and a half. After about two miles, you'll begin to understand why this is such a fine road. Starting with a fabulous series of esses running through the hills and canyons of the San Ynez Mountains, Highway 33 takes you gently by the hand, slowly introducing you to the more complex pavement.

On your right, at about the four mile mark, you'll see an imposing slice of granite called Nordoff Ridge. Bobby and I joke that this rocky form is really some sort of spooky stone god that watches over all good driving and riding enthusiasts. (Of course, Bobby and I have been known to, on occasion, sit around late at night and drink too much.)

Within five miles, Highway 33 begins to slice its way through a long series of canyons and gorges. For the most part, this road leaves out the nasty, tiring corkscrews that can make mountain excursions so tiring. Instead, you are left with miles of fast, easy curves that accommodate a wide range of driving skills.

There are problems with rockslides on the first half of Highway 33, but most are minor. When small slides do occur, they're usually found in the same spots, with permanently posted signs warning you of any trouble ahead. There always seems to be at least one stretch of Highway 33 that narrows down to one lane for both directions. But because traffic is often light, delays longer than two or three minutes are rare,

Don't forget that this highway is very narrow in spots and there's precious little shoulder to cushion you should you lose concentration. But because it is a well-designed road, it rarely makes you feel anxious. To the contrary, this road has a way of instilling confidence in good drivers and riders. Those possessing a goodly amount of skill should be able to hustle through most of these rocky corridors with ease.

Several changes in elevation add to the fun of this highway. Starting near the 750 foot level, you'll climb to 3,000 feet by the 12 mile mark, reaching a peak of 5,084 feet at Pine Mountain Summit—about 30 miles into our journey. Rarely does the ascent feel laborious. Instead, Highway 33 treats you to a smooth upward rise.

About 25 miles out, the road runs along Sespe Creek. Though dry for most of the year, it provides five miles of enjoyment as you scoot along the contours of this riverbed. Off to your right quarter will be Pine Mountain—looking more like a range of mountains—running for a good 15 miles along Highway 33. It's an interesting looking mountain where huge rocks jut out towards the road in an array of shapes and formations that's amazing and fascinating.

The remaining terrain is often covered with chaparral and scrub brush, the staple vegetation for areas like this. Unfortunately, you'll continue to see evidence of the fire that ravaged hundreds of acres along much of the first 20 miles of Highway 33. The hardy chaparral continues to grow back, but many of the small trees and bushes had no defense against the oncoming blaze. Thankfully, the slow healing process can be seen in progress on many of the hills and mountainsides.

At around the 30 mile mark you're in for the most breathtaking view offered by Highway 33. Pine Mountain Summit, at just over 5,000 feet, commands a stunning look at Cuyama Valley and expansive Los Padres National Forest. Full of great heights and vistas of the surrounding landscapes, it's a view that holds little evidence of intrusion by man. Numerous turnoffs, at a variety of elevations, enable you to enjoy the views on your way down from the summit, too.

Moving downwards, Highway 33 uses a handful of switchbacks and fiesty twists to get to the floor of Cuyama Valley. It's easily the most challenging and demanding passage of the trip. Lasting less than five miles, it's quite steep at times as you drop about 2,500 feet. And with so few of the turns posted with curve speeds, caution is advised.

As you make your final descent into Cuyama Valley, you'll look back with fond memories of the road just traveled. This first stretch of Highway 33 is mountain driving at its best—feeding the hungry enthusiast a constant variety of curves and twists set into a wide range of topography and scenery. One moment you're riding on little hills, fast sweepers the next, followed by big 180 degree turns that hug the shoulders of canyon after canyon. This is serious stuff. It's hard to find fault with the first 35 miles of Highway 33.

Moving north, you'll find the turnoff leading to Interstate 5 clearly marked, and it's near this point that Highway 33 begins to change. First, you'll find the mountains and foothills moving away from the road, having little influence on its course as it enters Cuyama Valley. Instead, the Cuyama River, always to your left, will be your guide for the next 15 miles. At times you'll ride just feet from its usually dry banks—its sandy, sun-baked bottom contributing little to the scenery.

From a driver's point of view, the course is straighter and more level. But, as we all know, that doesn't mean the fun has to stop. Waiting for you are several batches of fast, easy curves joining with more than one tight wiggle of road—all seemingly designed to keep your spirit and reflexes up. The 40-45 mile leg is especially nice, with a combination of gentle curves and fast half mile straights supplying the entertainment.

Cuyama Valley is increasingly being reclaimed for agricultural purposes. Though not lush by any standards, it's not a bad place to be. Where the chaparral and scrub have failed to do their job, large expanses of earth and rock lay barren along the mountains that surround this valley. An occasional pine tree, looking strangely out of place, can be seen growing at the higher elevations of these rocky peaks.

At about the 45 mile mark, you'll trade Ventura County for Santa Barbara County. What's noteworthy is that the sign announcing the change also marks the starting line of one awesome straight. Running less than two miles, this straight slowly moves up about 25 feet in elevation. I've seen cars take this stretch going fast—very fast. I remember on one hot summer afternoon being passed by a black Corvette doing at least 140 mph. I'm certainly not recommending that you drive faster than the speed limit, but I know that long straights laid out like this one are hard for many enthusiasts to resist.

Watch for a rise after about a mile and a half on this straight as there are several driveways along here where cars pulling out can force you into shedding speed much quicker than you'd like. I'd slow down before the top of the rise, as most cars won't be able to see over it. Otherwise, visibility is very good. The only other problem I've seen on this section of Highway 33 is slow moving farm equipment using the road to get from field to field. Stay alert and you should have few problems.

About eight miles after entering Santa Barbara County, you'll enter another county, San Luis Obispo. Don't get the two county signs confused! San Luis Obispo County offers several treacherous stretches that make it very dangerous to continue any high speed high jinxs you might have been doing in Santa Barbara County. It's not bad at 55 mph, but if you're taking this at felony speeds, there are several short stretches where uneven pavement is capable of creating havoc for even the best handling cars and motorcycles.

The worst offender is a one mile stretch just past the "ENTERING SAN LUIS OBISPO COUNTY" sign. Trust me on this one. You can't see the unevenness—but it's treacherous. It can take a car or motorcycle and move it in ten different directions—all in just a few feet. It is the driver's equivalent of a swimmer's riptide; you can't really see it—but it can quickly put you in a crisis situation. Unlike the beach, there are no lifeguards to protect you.

The last few miles of Highway 33 consist of smooth straights joined by long, easy doglegs that allow a finish at relatively high speeds. A stop sign at about 55 miles concludes our trek at the junction of Highway 166.

A left turn on Highway 166 will take you towards Santa Maria and the small towns of Cuyama and New Cuyama. (They're just too busy farming out here to take the time to think up new town names.) Turning right will point you in the direction of Bakersfield. Plus, you'll also be able to pick up Highway 33 again after about five miles on Highway 166. Highway 33 runs in a northerly direction for about 100 miles, much of it along the Temblor Range. Unfortunately, it manages to cover some of the uglier landscape California has to offer. I don't recommend it unless the sight of creaking oil rigs is high on your must-see list.

One other note of interest: parts of Highway 166 are very straight, especially the six mile stretch into Cuyama. Again, I've seen cars take this smooth, well behaved pavement at extremely high speeds. You can get something to eat or drink in the Cuyamas, though I have nothing in particular to recommend there.

I like Highway 33. Its remoteness keeps it relatively free of traffic—which for the enthusiast, only increases this byway's attraction. A disproportionate number of the vehicles traveling this road are high performance autos and motorcycles, most from nearby Santa Barbara and Ventura—and usually that's a good indication of a road's worthiness.

It can get very warm during the long summer months on Highway 33—especially the run through Cuyama Valley—so you'd be wise to carry water with you. In addition, there are no gas or repair services available for miles at a time on this highway, so be sure to tank up before you begin your excursion. And, I'd be shirking my duties as an enthusiast if I failed to mention that the patrol is usually very light on Highway 33, with the only known hot spot the first five miles outside of Ojai.

In closing, I have one request. If you're ever out on Highway 33 and see a sleek black sport bike and a stealth-like Porsche running tandem, just pull over and let 'em by. You see, Bobby and I love this road and when we finally get a chance to drive it together, we'll do it with an unbridled passion that's best left undisturbed. Guys like Bobby and me just don't know how to do it any other way...

Highway 41

Direction: Northeast.
Distance: About 45 miles.
Driving time: From two to three hours.
Congestion: Light. Medium around Atascadero.
Road condition: Average.
Patrol: Light.

This circuit escorts you from the small fishing port of Morro Bay, through rugged coastal ranges, on towards Atascadero and into the exhilerating foothills lying to the east. It serves up some inspiring blacktop along with plenty of impressive scenery in a little-known region of California. This road stands for fun, whether your travel be at legal speeds or beyond.

Highway 41 starts at one of my favorite seaside towns, Morro Bay. This area continues to draw travelers using its picturesque harbor, fine beaches, and superb sportfishing as lures. Its attractive horizon is crowned with one of Central California's most famous landmarks, Morro Rock, rising 576 feet out of the surf. And with three of the roads in this guide commencing within a 15 mile radius (Highways 1, 41 and 58), it makes an ideal destination for the serious enthusiast. (You'll find additional information on Morro Bay in the Highway 1 summary in the Central California section of this guide.)

You'll find Highway 41 beginning in Morro Bay off of Main Street, at the intersection where the Shell and Chevron gas stations are located. Within a half mile of departing town you'll be greeted by a 55 mph speed limit. Before the road lifts you into the coastal ranges, a quick glance back towards the west will reward you with one last dazzling glimpse of Morro Rock.

The opening miles of Highway 41 wriggle up the base of the hills that fringe the eastern side of Morro Bay. But these uplands create few ripples in the pavement, instead offering a fairly straight, though upward path. Much of the roadside scenery is determined by what the local farmers have planted along this first section of roadway.

About five miles into our journey, a right-left combination, posted at 40 mph, opens the road to more adventurous motoring.

For several miles this stretch employs an increasingly rigorous track as it begins to scale the peaks in a more stimulating fashion. You'll continue to rise until about the 12 mile mark, where you'll top out at 1,440 feet.

At about the nine mile mark, you'll pass the Halfway Station, where the road reverts back to straighter ways, Several of these asphalt arrows are long enough to pass slower traffic—if you've got an ample supply of horses at your command. There's nothing remarkable about the remaining eight or so miles to Atascadero, just high-gear highway that combines medium curves with short straights through pleasant, if not spectacular scenery. Unfortunately, this stretch of Highway 41, between Morro Bay and Atascadero, can get heavy with traffic since it's the fastest way to north Highway 101 from the coast. Sadly, only when traffic is light does this leg of Highway 41 show the traveler a good time.

After invading the western outskirts of Atascadero at about the 13 mile mark, speed limit signs urge you to hold your forward momentum to 45 mph. At the first traffic light after passing under Highway 101, you'll need to make a left turn onto El Camino Real. From there you'll stutter through the central business district for about a half mile before making a right turn. This busy community, about 16 miles into our journey, offers plenty in the way of food, gas, and lodging. Unfortunately, the lack of direction signs doesn't help in figuring out an already confusing course that zigzags through the eastern outskirts of town. (I strongly suspect local folks have a penchant for green and white Highway 41 road signs.)

Within two miles of passing Highway 101, our roadway sheds most traces of civilization. Traffic lights and revolving fast food signs are replaced with bucolic horse farms and cattle ranches. Plenty of stopping places exist for those who want a closer look at the fine collection of four-legged animals inhabiting the roadside.

By the 20 mile mark, you'll be into the foothills that make this region a haven for motoring enthusiasts. And because it's not a popular route, traffic lightens considerably upon leaving Atascadero's east flank. You'll also notice a change in terrain as the hills squeeze a few more slants into their silhouettes. The pavement reflects this geographical remodeling by becoming an upward pull at times. At its extreme, the road employs tight turns with top speeds nearing 15-20 mph—turns so coiled they seem to take but a heartbeat to complete. But for the most, it's not a torturous, corkscrew path requiring an endless series of arm-twirling maneuvers. Instead, this association with winding road produces a selection of mostly well behaved twists that ably serve the serious enthusiast.

Around 25 miles out, you'll eye the Chevron pumping station.

Right after passing this foul looking facility (little effort is made by Chevron to cover up the unsightly buildings and storage tanks), you'll be introduced to pavement that traverses a hillier section of highway, adding to the spirited nature of this already entertaining stretch. Built with just enough straights to keep you from feeling like you're wrestling with an endurance course, Highway 41 reaps plenty of points here.

Within five minutes of leaving Chevron's unsightly berth, the landscape takes on a more desolate appearance. And like partners in crime, the pavement becomes much less predictable as one minute it runs straight as a plumb over squat hills, while the next few ticks of the timepiece bring with them a bundle of curves and esses. Those with an affinity for diversity will love this piece of roadway.

But the finest section of Highway 41 is the 30-to-40 mile leg. Here, this tumultuous roadway sticks tight to the contours of the hills, offering up a myriad of compass changes, cracking you from corner to corner like an amusement park ride gone mad. Some curves are built on hills in such a way so that while your car is fighting momentum in one direction—often while at the apex of the curve—you're introduced to another force in an entirely different direction. Fun, fun, fun.

Those driving with the intent of taking no prisoners are guaranteed to find themselves scrambling for traction more than once on this stretch. Half-witted drivers will find themselves doing more plowing than a farmer at harvest time. Luckily, there are plenty of straights to catch your breath, though most are much too short for passing should you encounter traffic (highly unlikely). And would it really surprise you that such safety features as guardrails are as rare as gas stations on this streak of asphalt?

Much of the credit for the bewitching personality of this leg of Highway 41 must go to the wicked little hills. Their substantial contribution frequently makes this road a joyous, heart-thumping experience. But use caution. If you're taking this stretch at anything resembling near flat-out, then these arced knolls can quickly become the enemy—often limiting your vision of the next curve to a preview that's seldom more than milliseconds in length. Slowly, this high-kicking ten mile stretch unravels, straightening up (though still quite hilly) as you close in on 40 miles of travel.

The terrain on this fiesty 30-40 mile leg is streamlined—devoid of most trees or large shrubbery. A stillness permeates the grassy foothills, making for a most quiescent landscape. The low rumble of an occasional vehicle roaming this path can be heard miles before it's seen. The lamentful bellowing of a lonesome cow seems to be the only murmur these muted grounds give up with any regularity. Sadly, there aren't a lot of places to pull off since the shoulders on this stretch of Highway 41 tend to be narrow—when they exist at all.

After a long straight leaps-frogs over a series of diminutive hills, you'll make a right turn at a stop sign, and then head east. The last few minutes point towards the small community of Shandon, a gritty little town tucked into the wrinkles of the foothills. I suggest—for reasons noted later—that you continue on another five miles to a tiny place named Cholame. That would put you near the junction of Highway 46, about 45 miles from our starting point of Morro Bay.

Much of the asphalt on this road is not in the best condition. Although many repairs have been done, the quality of those mends is suspect in places. This is a road overdue for major resurfacing. Don't worry—I'm not talking Coupe De Ville-size potholes and gullies capable of swallowing up vast legions of autos and sportbikes—but I would advise you to keep extra alert for the ruts and wrinkles that dot this roadway.

The posted curve speed advisory information on much of Highway 41 is not as good as I'd like. Some of the tighter twists are marked with speed advisories, while others are not, leaving the traveler with little advance warning on what to expect.

Patrol by the local police and the CHP is extremely light east of Atascadero. In Atascadero, the local authorities troll in blue and white patrol cars, doing their best to keep an eye on people like you and me. You can expect patrol between Morro Bay and Atascadero (CHP) to range from light to medium.

Highway 41 reminds me a bit of Highway 58, a sizzling arrangement of asphalt running a few miles south of Highway 41's course. Because of their close proximity, they tend to have similar terrain and scenery, the important difference being that Highway 41 sports a less treacherous (and less intimidating) lineup of curves and twists. When I have a few days to spend motoring in this area, I often use Highway 41 as a warmup before taking on the more demanding Highway 58.

Any serious discussion of this highway would be incomplete without covering a tragic incident that took place on September 30, 1955. Late that warm afternoon, near a small dot on the map called Cholame, a rare Porsche 550 Spyder shot west on old Route 466 on a high speed shakedown run. Purchased new the week before from a dealership in Hollywood, its one hundred and ten horses roared out of a fiesty 1.5 liter air-cooled flat four. Wrapped in silver aluminum, adorned with the race number 130, it streaked like a serial numbered bullet towards Salinas to compete in a race scheduled for that weekend. In the passenger seat was the driver's German-born mechanic, Rolf Wutherich.

Driving was a young, little-known actor from Indiana named James Dean.

As he put the lightweight rocket, agile and fast, through its paces about a mile east of Cholame, a young student heading home to Fresno eased his burly 1950 Ford into the intersection of Highways 41 and 466, directly into the path of the speeding Porsche. In a savage, violent meeting of solid American steel and the German car's delicate aluminum, the small, low slung Porsche became the target, with the driver's side absorbing much of the impact. The mechanic, thrown free, would live another 25 years before dying on a rain soaked highway near his birthplace in Germany. James Dean would not be so lucky. He would cling to life for a few minutes before succumbing to his multiple injuries.

The following month, the movie *Rebel Without A Cause* premiered, with James Dean electrifying the masses with his portrayal of an angry and troubled young man. Just weeks later, *Giant,* featuring his final screen performance, would be unleashed on, what was by now, a Dean-hungry public, further cementing this young man's quick transformation from idol to icon.

The crumpled Spyder's aluminum body was sent on a nationwide tour, evidently intended to be a sobering reminder of what speed can do, proving that no one—not even one seemingly invincible—is immune when the combined forces of steel and horsepower go awry.

Old Route 466 is closed now, making it difficult to pinpoint that fatal intersection. For those seeking something tangible—a place to pay your respects—a monument was placed in front of Cholame's tiny post office in 1977. The stainless steel shrine, its mirror-like surface reflecting the road lying just feet away, has a simple inscription listing the facts: name, date of birth, and date and time of death. A gnarled Tree of Heaven towers over this simple tribute. Japanese sea pebbles, considered good luck, are scattered about like loose change at the bottom of a wishing well.

A few miles northeast lies a less obvious, though no less important shrine. Tucked behind a barbed wire fence are the decaying remains of an old, narrow two-laner designated Route 466. Rotting wood and board guardrails mark the sharpest curves of a path that long ago lost its graceful lines and angles. A faded, dog-eared trail that seems to poignantly reflect not only that young man's joy of the open road, but sadly, his fate too.

Highway 49

Direction: North.
Distance: About 315 miles.
Driving time: Two to three days.
Congestion: Light to moderate.
Road condition: Easily the best in this guide.
Patrol: Light, except around major towns.

By cutting a most agreeable path through a region known as the Gold Country, Highway 49 captures the colorful history of this great state unlike any other highway. With the discovery of gold in 1848, thousands flocked to California in the hope of striking it rich—a migration that seems to continue unabated today. It's an area whose rich and storied past played a significant role in developing California.

Highway 49 offers the driving and riding enthusiast plenty of good driving—including a satchel of great back roads and country lanes running off this entertaining path. Highway 49, with it's combination of picturesque scenery and historical atmosphere, makes for a unique itinerary.

We begin our journey in the town of Oakhurst. This mountain community is home to a hodgepodge of fast food places, gas stations, and tacky little shops. Looking like zoning run amuck, Oakhurst looks out of place in these lovely mountains. Fortunately, by making a turn at the Exxon gas station, you quickly leave the urban sprawl after only a mile or so.

On the 27 mile leg from Oakhurst to Mariposa, you'll drive through scenic foothills dotted with pine and oak. Traffic will be moderate for the first five miles. After passing through the small town of Ahwahnee you'll have several nice views of the Stanislaus National Forest off to your right. These beautifully forested mountains and valleys are sure to please the eye.

The road from Oakhurst to Mariposa acts as a slow warm-up for the skilled enthusiast. Offering little in the way of difficult pavement, you'll find most stretches filled with easy, medium curves connected to straights of sufficient length to usually allow passing of any traffic you've encountered. While traveling this section, you'll hit several steep grades, all well marked. The steepest downhill drop is just after entering Mariposa County, around the ten mile mark. Even when not on inclines, Highway 49 remains a hilly course consisting of wide curves matched with an occasional tighter turn. The asphalt is in excellent condition throughout this section.

This first stretch of Highway 49 ends at the city of Mariposa. Since Mariposa lies halfway between Merced and Yosemite National Park, it can get fairly crowded, especially on the weekends. You'll find plenty of historical buildings in this southernmost town of the Gold Country region. The best known is the two-story wooden courthouse (it's on your right) easily seen from Highway 49. It's the oldest functioning courthouse in California. As you leave town, watch for the left turn you'll need to make to stay on Highway 49.

Leaving Mariposa won't bring a lot of changes in terrain. You'll enter a less mountainous region, but the road stays much as it was before Mariposa, with wide, easy curves built on occasionally steep grades. Between Mariposa and the community of Bear Valley, you'll find plenty of pleasant scenery consisting of rolling foothills dotted with oak trees. It's the type of landscape that's synonymous with the Gold Country, and you'll see it often as you explore the lower elevations of Highway 49.

About a mile out of Bear Valley, Highway 49 begins a dramatic change starting with a four mile descent into a long valley. There's a view point on your left where you can take pictures of the lovely valley you'll soon be driving through. You'll also glimpse the Merced River just before it empties into Lake McClure. This marks the beginning of the most desolate stretch of Highway 49; combining great heights and vistas with little sign of man's intrusions.

As Highway 49 receives encouragement from the rugged landscape, you'll find plenty of switchbacks and wicked corners whipping you through this passage. Many turns don't have guardrails, and some of the drops are well over a thousand feet, so use plenty of caution if you decide to take this downward spiral aggressively.

Anytime you combine hairpin curves with steep grades you're asking for trouble, causing problems for even the most skilled enthusiast. Ivory tower drivers and riders would be smart to take this stretch slowly—if they take it at all. Traffic is usually light and there are plenty of places to pull off for resting or picture taking. You'll reach the lowest point of this stretch about five miles past Bear Valley, while crossing over the Merced River.

As soon as you cross over the Merced River, Highway 49 quickly explodes upwards. Cutting a cantankerous path through mountains with a wild abandon, the pavement whips you in a hundred different directions—each more fun than the last. A complete arsenal of road tricks awaits—quick esses, nasty little switchbacks, funny twitches of road that defy description—this must be what heaven is like. Few of the twists on this stretch are marked with curve speed signs, and you'll find little protection in the shape of curbs or guardrails.

The views on this part of Highway 49 are pleasant, especially when gazing towards the west, where a beautiful valley rests. Around the 50 mile mark, you'll begin heading back down in elevation. The roadway offers up an occasional straight now, and by the time you reach the outskirts of the attractive little town of Coulterville, Highway 49 becomes much easier to handle. I'm usually so drained by the time I get to Coulterville that my body almost demands that I stop and rest or change drivers.

After Coulterville, Highway 49 continues to rely more on straights to take you north. Several long ones just above Coulterville move you effortlessly towards higher speeds. But your brief respite from the curly stuff is soon over as the spirited nature of Highway 49 returns in the form of a short spurt on winding downhill road—though not nearly as tight as the road between Coulterville and Bear Valley. You'll travel on road flanked by rocks and mountains; curiously, the only thing that's missing is the winding road signs.

North of Coulterville, Highway 49 travels through a seemingly endless number of canyons and ravines. The best stretch for riding and driving between Coulterville and Sonora is just past the bridge crossing over Moccasin Creek. It's some of the most perfect asphalt anywhere, consisting of a two mile swatch of sizzling esses made even better by being built using an undercarriage of small hills. It's pavement like this that brings new meaning to Highway 49's nickname: Mother Lode Highway. I've been on tracks that weren't as exciting as this piece of Highway 49. As you fly over these brash little hills towards the Moccasin Power House, only the strongest will be able to resist hurtling through this enthusiast's concoction of twists and turns.

Right after passing the Moccasin Power House, you'll meet up with Highway 120. Make a left turn to stay on Highway 49. You'll have covered over 60 miles at this point. While enjoying the scenic Moccasin Reservoir on the right hand side, Highway 49 straightens, with higher speeds attainable. As you head towards the community of Chinese Camp, the curves return in a wider, easier to handle form. Watch for a right turn near Chinese Camp that you'll need to make to stay on course.

Upon leaving Chinese Camp the terrain begins a slow trans-formation from mountainous landscapes to rolling foothills and grazing lands. It's an easy road, straight and smooth, and well-placed medium bends and curves do little to slow down the significant number of travelers exceeding the 55 mph limit by a good margin.

You'll also find traffic increasing, especially after the right turn at the junction of Highway 108, about seven miles from Sonora. The last five miles leading up to the city limits of Sonora are through a non-descript, semi-rural area, with the only interesting place being Jamestown, about four miles before Sonora. Jamestown is one of the first communities formed during the Gold Rush days and has a wonderful Old West look seen in the beautifully restored stone and wood-framed buildings lining its Main Street.

Sonora, our next stop, also has a sense of history permeating its streets and structures. Since it's one of the largest towns on Highway 49, you can find just about everything here—including traffic. It can be horrendous coming from either direction, but it's especially bad coming from the south. Be prepared to spend a little time in this bustling little city—whether you like it or not. I've stayed here often, but I don't have any great recommendations on lodging. (Though I'm sure the best watering hole in town lies in the dark recesses of the Sonora Inn.)

With plenty of traffic accompanying you as you leave Sonora, aggressive driving will become difficult. Do the best you can because the 16 miles between Sonora and Angels Camp is another great piece of road, much of it angling downward. Plenty of little hills add to the excitement, with the best run coiled into a little dash just after Carson Hill. It consists of just-tight-enough curves and twists that score high in the fun-to-drive department. Lovely foothills, serene grazing lands, old abandoned barns, tarnished mining relics—all come together to make the drive pleasant for the eyes, too.

Just minutes north of Sonora, you'll find the turnoff for one of the most historic stops on Highway 49. Columbia, now a State Historic Park, has successfully preserved the flavor of the Gold Rush era in a collection of restored and reconstructed buildings experienced by strolling its creaking, wooden boardwalks. You'll see the Wells Fargo office, churches, a firehouse, at least one saloon and more in this gem of the Mother Lode.

The town of Angels Camp will forever be associated with Mark Twain's classic story, *The Celebrated Jumping Frog of Calaveras County*. And, as you can imagine, the town has a Jumping Frog Jubilee every May at the county fairgrounds, near Frogtown (where else?). I was lucky enough to enter one year since renting frogs to out-of-towners is big business. Rules for the frog jumping contest are simple: you have three jumps to make your frog jump the farthest.

Unfortunately, on its first attempt my frog sat frozen at the starting line, imitating a green rock. A bit of prodding with my shoe convinced our little green friend to finally make a jump of, oh, maybe six inches. It then stopped—and with slight quiver, promptly died. And there the dead little sucker sat—less than a foot from the starting line—as all the other frogs clamored towards an exciting finish.

The little boy I had rented it from looked rather amused as I handed the limp, and by now, worthless frog back to him. Just a few minutes later I saw him renting a different frog to another unsuspecting tourist. I thought of sharing our experiences with the renter, but I held my tongue as I watched their frog win its heat in what seemed like near-record time.

Later in the day, we cheered up considerably after retreating to a nearby establishment for some liquid refreshment. After a few rounds, our makeshift wake had engulfed the small local bar, producing more than one reasonably poignant toast to our little friend that had, by now, been immortalized (at least in spirit) with the name of Ted the Dead Green Thing.

Anyway, I assure you that my experience with the local kids has done little to dampen my enthusiasm for Angels Camp. I think it's a good example of blending the old and the new into a reasonable harmony. Founded back in 1848, it sets almost 100 miles into our journey.

Our next leg of the Mother Lode Highway takes us from Angels Camp to Jackson, a distance of just under 30 miles. This slightly hilly road travels on wide, easy curves with generous shoulders, and is much tamer when compared to some of the previous stretches of Highway 49. Traffic is usually moderate, especially after leaving Angels Camp.

You'll find two cities between Angels Camp and Jackson. The first, San Andreas, adds little to our excursion while the quaintness of Mokelumne Hill can only be seen by taking the "HISTORIC" detour heading east off of Highway 49. I recommend that you take the extra time to explore the attractive collection of fine old houses and buildings spread along its lovely Main Street. The road comes right back to Highway 49, making this quick side trip to Mokelumne Hill easy and convenient.

Upon leaving Mokelumne Hill, you'll drive about eight miles to Jackson, the largest city in Amador County. Just a few miles north of Jackson lies Sutter Creek, certainly one of the most likeable towns in the Gold Country. Plenty of historical structures can be found along its Main Street. (It seems that every Gold Rush town has a Main Street, doesn't it?). This time, without detours, Highway 49 takes in many of the best sights Sutter Creek has to offer.

From Sutter Creek to Highway 50 is a distance of about 37 miles. You'll begin with a six percent grade that continues to move the traveler down in elevation. Up to this point, we've spent much of our journey in the 1,500-2,000 foot range. But once you reach Amador City, you'll be under the 1,000 foot mark for the first time on Highway 49.

Both Amador City and Drytown, about three miles north, have interesting histories. Despite its name, Drytown was not devoid of alcohol—quite to the contrary. Over two dozen saloons made it easy for the hard working miners to quench their hearty thirsts. The town actually got its name from a nearby dry creek. Amador City did better with mining quartz than gold, but today it's known more for its quaint shops rather than as a source of minerals.

Though much smaller than Sutter Creek, Amador City and Drytown are loaded with charm and make pleasant stops. Further north, the towns of Plymouth and Nashville have both seen better days, offering the traveler little in the way of services or scenery.

At the junction of Highways 49 and 12, you'll need to turn right to stay on Highway 49. This point is about 135 miles into our journey. There's little to report in regards to driving until you get north of Plymouth. From there, the road begins to cut and jag through oak covered hills, but it's a passage that makes few demands on the traveler.

One of the great strengths of Highway 49 is how it constantly changes scenery and terrain, seemingly offering new sights and landscapes around every bend. On this stretch you'll find a mixed bag of fun little hills, mountain driving, smooth straights, and even a corkscrew or two as you head north. The only drawback is a lack of straights long enough to pass the traffic you'll probably encounter.

The downward trend of the last few miles is thwarted as pieces of Highway 49 begin to head upwards near the 145 mile mark. The scenery, too, reflects the diversity of the last 20 miles. Grazing lands, mountains, foothills, and farms grace the path, making the miles roll effortlessly by.

As you close in on Placerville, you can expect traffic to increase. To stay on Highway 49 make a right turn at Poor Red's (best ribs for miles). You'll find plenty of congestion at this point so just take it easy on the remaining six miles before meeting Highway 50. You'll need to make a left (well marked) about two and a half miles past Poor Red's to stay on Highway 49.

Placerville, sitting at about the 155 mile mark, is the halfway point of our trek through the Gold Country. Many people stop here on the first day since this pleasant, though congested community offers a variety of places to stay and eat.

Once you cross over Highway 50, you'll find Placerville changing. The first two miles north of the main highway are through a residential section with moderate traffic. After that, Highway 49 thins out a bit as the road's outline gets a few more curves. It begins to run pell-mell through hills along an often narrow path. With plenty of small trees packed densely along the road, the eight miles from

81

Placerville to Coloma make for fun and scenic traveling. You'll find plenty of houses and farms spread along the first half of the Placerville-Coloma leg, while the second half is less populated and more secluded.

Coloma is where gold was first discovered back in 1848, setting off a course of action that would change California forever. Highway 49, running through Coloma, skirts along the south fork of the American River. A replica of Sutter's Mill stands on the banks of the river near where gold was discovered by James Marshall.

The 18 miles of road on the Coloma-Auburn leg combine a wide range of road surfaces. The path from Coloma to the little hamlet of Pilot Hill is made up of wide curves and smooth straights. But from Pilot Hill north to Auburn, the road becomes more entertaining. A good number of curve speed advisory signs reflect a change in emphasis from speed to finesse. An eight percent downward grade makes the going between the towns of Cool and Auburn especially fun.

The best section between Highway 50 and Auburn is the quick run just after you cross over the American River—heading left on a course that cuts a spirited path along the shoulder of a small mountain. Loads of oak trees provide scenic relief as you continue to course through the rolling foothills of the Mother Lode.

The section from Auburn to just north of Grass Valley is a popular but missable stretch of Highway 49. Auburn, the county seat of Placer County, is clogged with traffic since it's home to the junction of Interstate 80 and Highway 49. And leaving Auburn is rarely a solitary act since Highway 49 is the main corridor between Auburn and the community of Grass Valley.

The speed limit on the northern outskirts of Auburn is 50 mph. There's a passing lane a few miles past Auburn—just as you dash through an ill-placed traffic signal. This first section between Auburn and Grass Valley rides like a small freeway with almost continual straights and wide, easy bends. And, like a freeway, you'll have three exits to choose from if you wish to visit Grass Valley.

The scenery upon exiting Grass Valley is pleasant enough, filling the sides of the road with mountains covered in a variety of pine. About five miles north of Grass Valley, Highway 49 stops its urban behavior and returns to being an enthusiast's road. Look for a turnoff that reads, "DOWNIEVILLE LEFT LANE HIGHWAY 49". It's here that you'll find relief from what is undoubtedly the worst section of Highway 49, the run from Auburn to Grass Valley. But any road running over 300 miles is bound to have a few letdowns and Highway 49 is no exception. And it's not so much that these 30 miles are bad, it's just that up to this point, Highway 49 has spoiled the traveler with miles of enjoyable road.

As if offering an apology, Highway 49 quickly returns to being a first class enthusiast's road upon leaving Grass Valley. After about three miles of easy, smooth straights, you'll see the familiar winding road sign announcing that the next five miles are going to be good ones.

The road begins to get tighter and the straights shorter as you aim downwards. Winding through forested mountains, the views become majestic as you close in on Tahoe National Forest. You enter its boundaries about a mile past North San Juan, another great little mountain town. As you begin your assault on the Sierra Nevada mountain range, you'll start a consistent climb near Downieville that supplies some of the best scenery on the trip. Luckily, traffic disappears as you continue through a region of Highway 49 that's lightly populated. Since snow at the higher elevations in the winter months often closes this section of roadway, you're wise to make this last segment a warm weather experience.

You'll occasionally encounter brief stretches of straight road on the 45 miles between Nevada City and Downieville. But much of the road will be made up of smooth, medium turns and short straights. Passing will sometimes require several miles of patience.

About three miles into Sierra County you'll meet up with the Yuba River. By crossing over a bridge, the banks of this flowing tributary will be to your right. This beautiful river, acting like a symphony conductor, orchestrates the rugged granite mountains with the forests of pine and bigleaf maples into a concert of the most soothing proportions. Numerous opportunities exist to stop and enjoy this peaceful river, whether it be for just a quick picnic or a cold dip (and I do mean cold).

Initially, brief glimpes are all that you get of this rushing river— but as you continue on, the views begin to linger. In many spots you'll see evidence of past mining operations that have left tons of rock piled along the banks.

As Highway 49 continues to follow the Yuba River, the path becomes increasingly remote. The road stays in uniformly good condition and it continues to rank high in entertainment value as it faithfully takes a path carved by the Yuba River. On hand will be an ample supply of road, full of esses and bends—all running through the grand scenery of the Tahoe National Forest.

Our next town, Downieville is one of my favorite stops on Highway 49. This tiny hamlet, home to about 500, is a most charming place. Nestled deep in a region known as the Northern Mines area, it was created by the fever of gold discoveries in the nearby Yuba River.

Downieville is a town made for walking. Those with a sharp eye will see everything from the original town gallows to the present-day Sierra County Museum. Many of the buildings that line its crooked streets passed the century mark years ago. And the local people have a marvelous way of carrying on with business despite numerous visitors. For those seeking refreshments or a light snack, there's a good bakery near the one-lane bridge.

From Downieville you'll travel to a beautiful vista point (with a view only Stevie Wonder could miss) overlooking Sierra Valley. It's here, just past Downieville, that after 250 miles of skirting the western slopes of the great Sierra Nevada, Highway 49 finally begins a head-on assault on the huge blocks of granite making up California's biggest mountain range.

You'll continue to have first class scenery as you run through terrain combining forests and granite—all with the lovely Yuba River at your side. Though a rewarding path for the enthusiast, the spectacular scenery makes it likely that you'll spend more time admiring the wonderful views than the curvature of the road. And that's fine since little of this section is difficult to drive or ride. It has just enough curve and sway to it to make an interesting, yet undemanding course.

About 12 miles past Downieville, Highway 49 discovers yet another charming little village, Sierra City. You'll see a nice collection of lovingly restored homes and businesses without leaving Highway 49. With a population below 300, Sierra City seems to have more mountains than people. Just after leaving town keep an eye to your left and you'll spot the Sierra Buttes. These rocky mountains, crowned with nearly bald pinnacles, bring a stark beauty to the landscape. You'll continue to rise as you aim towards the high point of Highway 49, Yuba Summit. At an elevation of 6,701 feet, it lies about 275 miles into our journey.

After Yuba Summit, you begin a downward trek that gets increasingly tighter. Curve speed signs offer plenty of guidance as you travel this often twisty run. Once again, the driving experience gets overshadowed by what is surely the single best view on Highway 49. At first, all you'll sneak is an occasional peek through the tall stands of pine, but a vista point about four miles past Yuba Summit finally allows an unimpeded view at one of the most beautiful places in California, the Sierra Valley.

Conveniently placed information placards at this spectacular vista point provide insightful information on the wildlife, geology, and history of this wonderful place. In 1851, James Beckwourth smartly established a hotel and trading post that provided early travelers with everything from hay to dairy products.

We finish our descent to the valley floor by riding through the great smelling alfalfa fields of the Sierra Valley. Strung along this last portion of Highway 49 are little towns like Sattley, Sierraville, Loyalton, and finally Vinton, where Highway 49 ends after 315 captivating miles. These last 30 miles are in stark contrast to what we've previously seen on Highway 49. Instead of curves and bends induced by the foothills and mountains, we speed along flat, wrinkle-free grasslands.

Sitting at about 5,000 feet, this mountain valley is traversed by long straights that undoubtedly see triple digit speeds on a regular basis. It's a bit bumpy in places (nothing serious), but after miles of twists and turns, the sight of these long arrow-like threads of pavement make it difficult to keep the speed down. Some of the straights funnel down into tight turns (35-45 mph range), but all turns were clearly posted with curve speed signs the last time I was on this road. After passing under a railroad overpass (subway) you'll find Highway 49 coming to a close at a stop sign at the junction of Highway 70.

I've yet to see the CHP in sparsely populated Sierra Valley. The county sheriff makes occasional appearances in marked white cars— their heads topped with light colored, cowboy-like hats. But on this road you're more likely to run into a cow than local authorities.

In summary, Highway 49 offers smooth, clean, beautifully laid asphalt. In fact, no other road in this guide comes close to matching the overall quality of Highway 49's surface. And the CHP keeps a low profile on much of this byway, making for an even more enjoyable excursion.

Much of Highway 49's path was determined by events over a century ago. Tales abound that reflect the frustration of thousands whose dreams and aspirations, spurred by the luring descriptions of surefire riches, were never fulfilled. Many are sordid stories, full of violence and lawlessness, often fueled by the cruelty that strikes when different cultures clash in their attempt to melt and mesh into one.

Of course, other stories brim with heroism and bravery. But most simply replay the desire of common people to better themselves, to find a new life, a better life. Thankfully, many of the places and people along Highway 49 still hold onto that spirit.

And last, but not least, this region is filled with the sad tales that always accompany any quest for riches. James Marshall's, the man who first discovered gold at Sutter's Mill, is easily one of the most disheartening stories. He eventually lost all he had gained, dying an embittered man. His final years were spent in menial jobs that were often near where he first made the discovery that is said to have not only changed a state, but a country.

I'm glad to report that every town along Highway 49 has its own unique story to tell. A healthy supply of back roads carry the traveler to such little-known places as Rough and Ready, Rescue, and Dutch Flat, each having played a small, though important role during those wild, free-spirited times.

And finally, the vast array of unique photographic opportunities on Highway 49 can sometimes overshadow the driving and riding experience. Weatherbeaten barns and rusted old farming and mining equipment scattered about the landscape help to provide small clues about how people once lived. Rather than scar the landscape, these decaying monuments to the past, untouched by progress, gently remind us of how things once were. I guess that someday they'll all be gone, reclaimed by the earth, picked at by tourists, or just rusted away until little is left. But until then, Highway 49 will remain a special path few can resist.

Highway 58

Direction: East.
Distance: 70 miles.
Driving time: One and a half to three hours.
Congestion: Very light.
Road condition: Average to good.
Patrol: Amazingly light.

According to Greek mythology, many an ancient mariner met his fateful end against the rocks while lured by the sweet singing of a sultry, beautiful siren. I can't help but wonder if Highway 58 isn't camouflaged as some kind of modern-day equivalent, as this highway seems to have definite plans for any enthusiast who ventures on it.

In its quest for notoriety, Highway 58 will sail you over blind hills, whisk you down long straights, and hurtle your vehicle off of mountain slopes at speeds that will have your passengers checking their pants for wet spots. Hey, this is my kind of road.

And it almost killed me a few years back.

Yet, despite having a serious accident on this road, I often yearn to go back—to take this road and show it who's boss. My logical side knows that an attitude like that can get me killed. So when I'm on this road, I hold back just the smallest bit—my way of showing respect, I guess.

Anyone who dares treat Highway 58 lightly risks numerous confrontations with their own limits. On the other hand, driving this road can be absolutely intoxicating. It offers miles and miles of exciting, challenging pavement that often encourages nearly flat-out motoring.

I'd be surprised if you've heard of this road since much of it runs through an area of California that offers little in the way of interesting places or people. And despite the fact that nice places like Morro Bay, Atascadero, Paso Robles, and San Luis Obispo are all within a 20 mile radius of its start, few people find their way onto this remote highway.

In its entirety, Highway 58 crosses much of the width of California in an east-west direction. Beginning in the foothill community of Santa Margarita, Highway 58 runs about 250 miles, much of it coursing through drab and boring terrain before ending in the high desert at Barstow. Fortunately, the 70 or so miles chosen for this book make up the best of Highway 58, touching only a bit on the unsightly, and then only on the last few miles of our trip.

Because so few people have a reason to be on this highway, it often sits empty—no matter what time of day. And, as unbelievable as it sounds, I've never seen the CHP or the local authorities enforcing the speed limit on Highway 58, and believe me, I've spent a lot of time on this back road.

Highway 58 begins at Highway 101, a couple of minutes west of Santa Margarita. If you're traveling by way of Highway 101, the exit for Highway 58 in either direction is clearly marked. You'll drive about a mile on a short road that also functions as the main street for Santa Margarita. After passing through this humdrum town, a right turn will take you over the railroad tracks and into the foothills that cover much of this area.

Be sure to heed the road sign noting that there are no automotive services for the next 70 miles (that includes gas). If you need fuel, you can get it back in Santa Margarita at a friendly Mobil station located on Highway 58.

After traveling less than four miles, Highway 58 begins to sing a more luring song. You begin to encounter a slew of curves and turns, occasionally with odd, off-camber banking. The hills add their effect—making the first seven miles a real test of ability.

By the seven mile mark, the double nickel becomes easier to attain. The straights continue to be short as the road rises into the southern end of the Diablo mountain range—the first of several mountain ranges you'll encounter.

But after ten miles, Highway 58 settles down somewhat, offering up mostly easy medium to medium-tight curves. At times, the road levels, but other times, small hills sneak under the pavement, adding to the playfulness of this highway.

The scenery is nice too, with cattle and horses lazily grazing on the hills that lie on either side of the road. Working windmills, a rare sight these days, tower on top of wind-swept hills, slowly coming to life when the breeze finds their outstretched arms.

You'll leave the wrinkled terrain of the foothills several times to drop into valleys—but usually only for a mile or two before the pavement rises back into the foothills. Quarter mile straights are typical on the 20-30 mile leg, helping make the miles roll effortlessly by. Occasional tight stuff will keep it interesting but most curves can be taken at 55 mph without too much trouble.

Before reaching the 40 mile mark, Highway 58 offers up a series of high speed straights for your driving and riding pleasure. We're talking outlaw speeds here, folks. The first one is at about the 37 mile mark and runs for about a mile and a half before a left, posted at 35 mph, slows you down. The next straight follows immediately, running for about two miles, and brings into view the oddest sight on Highway 58: the Arco solar equipment located in always sunny California Valley. Look off to your left and you'll glimpse long rows of huge, shiny monoliths standing sentinel, diligently catching the sun's rays.

The third straight in our series runs less than a mile and runs by a small school—so use caution if you're passing it on a school day! Sloughing off speed, you'll be greeted by a tight, left turn posted at 15 mph. This next straight, at about the 42 mile mark, is the longest and must see triple digit speeds on a regular basis. All three straights in this series are in good shape, with only an occasional small bump marring the surface.

Straight road continues to be the main course, but now Highway 58 begins to throw little 15 to 20 foot hills onto the pathway. Approaching these hills at a fast pace makes flight *more* than just a possibility. As you soar blind over each one, this siren-like course gives the aggressive driver and rider a gut-wrenching workout. All the dips and dives will make you wonder if the sound of your pounding heart isn't the first verse of some alluring melody—a melody that's sure to lead you into the darkest folds of this desolate land.

Each crest leads to another, more furious hill. This blitz will continue unabated for about three miles, though smaller rises are spread out all along this stretch of Highway 58. Maybe the builders of this road decided to leave them intact because the San Andreas Earthquake Fault runs through here. Whatever the reason, they add much to the enjoyment of this road.

A right turn, just short of the 50 mile mark, takes Highway 58 through the flat plains and grasslands of a remote area known as the Carrizo Plain. By this time, you'll begin to notice a range of mountains looming ahead. These are the slopes of the Temblor Range, soon to sweep you to a summit of 3,258 feet.

Leaving the flatlands behind, you'll rise over 1,000 feet on a most interesting and challenging mountain run. It's the most dangerous and difficult section of Highway 58. As the road begins to wrap itself around the smooth, rounded mountains, it uses medium to medium-tight curls to take the first few miles. Many will find the banking odd and hard to figure. Decreasing radius turns are everywhere and there's little in the way of guardrails, plus the road constantly narrows and widens.

There's something about this mountain course that I find exhilarating. Sucking me in like few roads do—forcing me to go progressively faster; each turn tighter than the one before. As I fight for more speed—while at the same time trying to find more control—I constantly feel for the small edge needed to safely take the countless swerves and curves.

I run these mountains in the highest rpm's my engine will let me get away with. Losing nerve and lifting off the throttle in some of the tighter curves can mean a quick visit to unpaved territory. And the small amount of shoulder on this section adds little room for error. This is unforgiving road—making it imperative that you get it right first time, every time. Numerous trick curves, blind crests, and a variety of cutthroat pavement make this section very, very demanding. (And, need I mention, very, very fun.)

Much of the run through the Temblor Mountains is with an embankment on your right, while off to your left wait drops of anywhere from 20 to 200 feet into flood-scarred ravines. You'll find loose gravel in many spots, but not bad enough to mess up paint jobs, though it can play havoc with traction.

And, by the way, we haven't even started to describe the back side of this mountain stretch. Winding road signs simply don't do the eastern side of this mountain run justice. It's as if a new, more severe sign was needed for this run. (Maybe a winding road sign with a set of jaws on it.) Few curve speed signs are available to help you gauge the many tight, twisty paths that this road takes moving downwards. Constantly curling back on itself, this road's torturous corkscrews push you stubbornly into tight 180 degree turns, as if it was making a game out of which direction to take next. Going up or going down, it doesn't matter—this mountain range is delightfully relentless.

By the 60 mile mark, you'll have begun your descent out of the Temblor Range. At last you'll have a few straights as Highway 58 enters Little Santa Maria Valley. To your left, grazing land will reappear; to your right lay hills covered with the odorous facilities utilized in the refining and storage of oil. And, of course, no oil drilling area would be complete without the endless parade of dinosaur shaped oil pumpers.

Thank goodness the last ten miles have several high speed straights, as this area easily has the worst scenery of our trip. (My honest opinion is that this stretch has no scenery.) The road dips and dives easily as it runs between nice long straights, making the increasingly arid landscape a bit more bearable.

All in all, Highway 58 is a thoroughly enjoyable road. The slalom through the Temblor Range, lasting less than ten miles, is preceded by 50 miles of wonderful, twisting, winding road through oak-studded foothills and mountains. The run finishes with another fun ten miles of road, though the view could best be described as about as enjoyable as ants in your kitchen.

You'll end up in a coarse little town known as McKittrick. All I can say about this place is that it smells and looks uglier than just about any other town I know of in California. (McKittrick will never show up in one of those oil company TV commercials touting the ecological achievements of the company and its workers). You either have to be crazy or be making *a lot* of money to be living here. For those who want to connect up with Interstate 5, just follow the road signs in McKittrick. From there it's a quick 16 miles to Interstate 5.

The pavement on Highway 58 is in reasonably good condition. In the early miles, serious repaving performed on several short stretches in late 1986 makes the going smooth and pleasant. And the other miscellaneous repair work done along Highway 58 is commendable. Only the run through the Temblor Range has a bit of spotty asphalt. On occasion, the mountain portion of our trek is bothered by small rock slides, but in most cases the debris is minor and easily missed.

It's a shame that Highway 58 doesn't lead somewhere interesting. But, on the other hand, I guess that's what keeps this road so free of traffic. If driving one of the premier chunks of pavement in California interests you, I'd make a beeline for this great highway.

Hopefully, you'll have better luck at taming this highway than I did.

Highway 140

Direction: East and north.
Distance: About 65 miles.
Driving time: From two to four hours.
Congestion: Light to moderate.
Road condition: Good.
Patrol: Light to moderate.

There's a road I know that winds through wooded canyons and gorges—its scenery blessed by the lovely Merced River flowing untamed along much of the path. Using fast straights and fun seeking curves to roam landscapes ranging from farmlands to granite peaks, this highway finishes its task by dropping you at the doorstep of one of America's most beautiful national parks.

Welcome to Highway 140.

We begin in the San Joaquin Valley at Merced. Located at the junction of Highways 99 and 140, this farming community often bills itself as the "Gateway to Yosemite". Despite that label, traffic on most of Highway 140 is usually light to moderate, even in the summer months.

You'll need about five miles of asphalt before you lose most signs of civilization on Highway 140. Getting to the eastern outskirts of Merced is done on road that's straight and level. With traffic often moderate, these even ribbons of pavement will come in handy for passing. But even without the excuse of passing traffic, speeds often escalate on this portion of Highway 140. Meanwhile, miles of treeless farmlands stretch out on either side of the road. Corn, almonds, and tomatoes are just a few of the crops grown in this fertile region of California.

The first community after Merced is Planada, about eight miles into our trek. The section of Highway 140 around Planada was resurfaced recently, making this a smooth road to travel on. The road begins to traverse small hills, though much of it remains straight as an arrow. Again, there's little here to slow your speed down. After Planada, crop lands turn to grazing lands and Highway 140 aims you towards the rolling foothills that lie to the east.

Upon entering Mariposa County (at about the 15 mile mark), the road begins to develop a more sporting personality as easy bends

92

soon give way to progressively more curvaceous road. The oak covered foothills become a more prominent part of the landscape, forcing Highway 140 to take additional chances as it edges ever closer to the Sierra Nevada.

By the time you reach the 20 mile mark, you'll be firmly entrenched in the foothills. And though the road still offers up stretches where the double-nickel can be exceeded, passing becomes more difficult as the hills often cut into your forward vision. Fortunately, strategically placed passing lanes on the 15-30 mile leg make life on Highway 140 a safer and more orderly venture.

The small community of Catheys Valley is about 25 miles into our journey. Many of its 300 residents find a cool respite from the hot summer heat at a small store sitting at the junction of Highway 140 and Hornitos Road. (More about Hornitos Road later.) By the time you reach Catheys Valley, you'll have climbed over 1,300 feet since Merced. It's been a very gradual, almost imperceptible climb to this point. But soon after leaving this small community the road becomes steeper. One of the best views on Highway 140 is from the foothills north of Catheys Valley. After passing the small Sun-Set Rock Shop, you'll have a splendid panorama of San Joaquin Valley as it shimmers then disappears into the western horizon.

The eight miles from the Sun-Set Rock Shop to Mariposa consist of road rolling through scenic hills and canyons with an easy summit thrown in for good measure. Traffic will invariably pick up as you head into Mariposa. A nice collection of medium curves—few difficult—makes up the last miles into Mariposa. The road is in good shape and lightly patrolled, adding to the pleasure of this highway.

Mariposa, about 37 miles into our journey, lies just beyond the halfway mark. This county seat has the oldest courthouse in California dating back to 1854. I don't find this bustling community particularly interesting—plus there are plenty of other towns sprinkled throughout the Gold Country that better reflect the history of this era. But, there's plenty of good food and lodging in Mariposa. Though with Highway 49 also running through town, you'll usually find this stop full of traffic and people.

Upon leaving Mariposa, Highway 140 loses some of its good manners. Beginning with several steep climbs, the pavement rises over a thousand feet in only four miles before it reaches Midpines Summit. From there, you head downwards on steep, but well built road. You'll notice the oak foothills have given way to steep mountains covered in different varieties of pine and cedar. The road from Mariposa to Midpines mainly consists of short quarter mile straights connected to medium to wide curves. Though not a hilly road, the elevation continues to seesaw as we head north on

Highway 140.

A couple of miles past Midpines, you'll see a sign reading, "STEEP WINDING GRADE NEXT 3 MILES". This downward spiral, full of switchbacks and tight twists, chooses a path through the mountains with scenery that seems bigger than life—the road flanked by giant chunks of granite growing ever larger—as if these mountains refused to lay dormant. Passing through Midpines, Highway 140 finally begins to level off, though plenty of good driving and attractive scenery remain.

The last 20 miles of Highway 140 surely offer the best scenery. The road is built along the banks of the beautiful Merced River. This river feeds famous Yosemite and Bridal Vail Falls from several of its forks. Flowing southwest, it finally empties into the San Joaquin River, back towards San Joaquin Valley. Every arc and bend exposes you to a different vision, gracefully combining river, mountain, and forest into moving portraits of great beauty. And with its banks full of shady spots, the Merced River makes a strong argument for picnicking. Plus, numerous turnouts act like waiting invitations, making it easy to stake out part of this scenic river for your own special moments.

The final 20 miles present challenging pavement in very good condition. Luckily our path faithfully follows the contours of the Merced River. With just-long-enough straights to pass slower traffic, you'll find this well paved section of Highway 140 holding plenty of medium to medium-tight curves. Occasionally, tighter turns make scrambling an option, but the road levels considerably, especially when compared to the ups and downs of the roadway out of Mariposa.

The final two miles of Highway 140 rest inside Yosemite National Park, where as you can imagine, the scenery gets even better. You'll run with a short stone wall that acts as your guide along this narrow stretch of asphalt. Huge boulders lean precariously towards you, making you wonder if this piece of road had anything more than a crumbling grip on the mountain walls. These last two miles are tight, fiesty pavement, making for a most fitting end to a marvelous highway.

Our trek finishes at the Arch Rock entrance station of Yosemite National Park. Beyond this point lies more of one of America's premier parks. Needless to say, this is a place where you'll want to spend some time. Though much has been written about Yosemite, I can't resist mentioning that this *really* is one of the most beautiful places on earth. Despite numerous visits, I'm always amazed at the great concentration of beauty that Mother Nature has bestowed on this small valley.

By now, it's obvious that I'm the type of traveler that's always eager to find new roads and places. An excursion off of Highway 140 paid big dividends one hot day when I discovered a small, out-of-the-way back road named Hornitos Road. You'll find this gem just south of Catheys Valley. The road, as its name implies, leads into Hornitos, which is probably the most realistic portrayal of what a hundred year-old gold rush town looks like when no one tries to make things "nice" for the tourist crowd. Sadly, because it's off the beaten path, few people find this honest old town nestled into the foothills.

Hornitos Road gets you to Hornitos in about nine miles. It then continues for about 11 more miles through rolling foothills unpopulated by people or cities. This 20 mile excursion ranks as one of the great back roads in California. Many enthusiasts who give Hornitos Road a whirl come back describing it as the best back road in California. At just 20 miles in length, it's too short to qualify for this guide—otherwise it would be included.

This fun back road cuts through the rolling hills in a mischievous and disorderly fashion. Made with only the finest curves and twists, Hornitos Road will bring out the spirit of the open road in anyone. The few locals who drive this road seem to know it well and take it almost as fast as the enthusiast. And, with pavement in reasonably good condition, this is a side trip I'd heartily recommend.

Looking at the facts, it's easy to see that spending time on Highway 140 pays impressive benefits. Those with an hour or two to spare while heading to or from Yosemite have Hornitos Road waiting. And since you're in a region crisscrossed with great back road nuggets, spending a day looking for your own Hornitos Road can bring hours of joy to those who love the open road. By combining lovely scenery with great chunks of pavement, it's easy to understand why Highway 140 is the enthusiast's favorite route to Yosemite.

Hwy 154 (San Marcos Pass)

Direction: Northwest.
Distance: About 32 miles.
Driving time: Half hour to an hour.
Congestion: Medium to heavy.
Road condition: Good.
Patrol: Light.

I have a friend named Nigel who's in commodities. Anyone with an inkling of that business knows that the burnout rate is high due to the massive amounts of stress and tension that come with the prospect of making or losing a fortune every time you trade. While having dinner together on one of his infrequent trips down to L.A., I found Nigel feeling a bit down, and I asked him why.

He said, "Well, I made two hundred thousand dollars before noon today."

"Nigel," I asked, "how could you be so down after that?"

He replied with a shrug, "Because after lunch I lost it all—plus another fifty."

Nigel was very much the quintessential modern day enigma. After ten years in an intense business, he had outlasted most of his peers with nary an emotional scar. His ability to cope with the wins and loses of life without the aid of drugs, therapy, and all the other so called *essentials* of modern life made him a legend among his friends.

One day while attending a house warming party at his beautiful new home just north of Santa Barbara, I pulled him aside and asked him what his secret was. Saying nothing, he motioned for me to follow him out towards the garage.

Now for as long as I'd known Nigel, he had always been given to high drama, and it appeared that this little scene would be no different. Moving at the tempo of a caged animal just set free, he quickly aimed the remote control not at the door of the main garage, but instead at a much smaller garage set off to the side of the driveway.

As the remote's radio waves did their job, the garage door slowly arced upwards with a metallic-like groan. As the small, darkened room flooded with light, my eyes darted along the outline of something sleek, something stealth-like.

It was a Ferrari Boxer.

Red? Hell, this thing was painted the most *impatient* red I'd ever seen

Later, while leaning against one of this car's seductive curves, hands fidgeting all the while in his pockets, he spoke, "Life's little tragedies and battles take their toll. Fighting that sometimes leaves you with a pretty big wound."

He continues, "It's all in how you close the wound—that's the secret. A lot of people take on the insurmountable task of trying to heal the wound—me, man, I'm just happy to close it for a while."

"And in a car like this, on a road like San Marcos Pass, I find that my outlook immediately improves. It's as if the sense of speed, the growl of the engine, the almost instantaneous power and torque, all combine out there on that highway into a prescription that leaves me feeling charged up, renewed—like I can take on the world one more time. I guess a $60 an hour shrink would be cheaper, eh?"

Probably, but not nearly as fun.

So as Nigel would surely have it, we embark upon a journey along his favorite road, San Marcos Pass (also known as Highway 154) which begins at the northern outskirts of Santa Barbara, off of Highway 101.

As you exit Highway 101 and begin traveling north on Highway 154, you'll find two miles of uninspired viewing as track homes and vacant lots fill the roadside. But after a sweeping right turn, you'll enter Los Padres National Forest, where the scenery begins to take on a more agreeable look.

As you continue on, the terrain quickly moves from rolling foothills to a more mountainous environ within a few minutes. You'll soon find man's imprint more difficult to track as the landscape is now host to scrub and chaparral. At the higher elevations, scatterings of pine trees add to the flavor of this road.

For the serious enthusiast, this highway pays the biggest dividends in its first half. The influence that the foothills and mountains have on this road is now put to good use and the road thickens with countless esses and switchbacks. Flying from corner to corner, anyone in a well-suspended vehicle will find this path laid out in a most welcome manner. Luckily, few hairpins wait to slow your progress. And with the first five miles running at a decidedly upward slant, you'll find your confidence building as more and more of this highway's twists pass under your wheels.

Alas, this road can get a bit congested. Tourists slogging along this highway often slow things down as they creep towards that little bit of Denmark called Solvang. (You'll lose this group at the junction of Highway 246, located at about the 24 mile mark.) You'll also find the camper and trailer set well represented on Highway 154 as they make their way towards camping bliss at Lake Cachuma.

Unfortunately, it doesn't seem to matter what time you travel as traffic seems to range from moderate to heavy most times of the day or week. Typically, if you pass slower cars, you'll get open road for awhile, only to encounter additional stragglers as you continue on. There's not much you can do but try to pass safely, or do what I do: just pull over and wait for traffic to get a bit head of me. Then I take to the throttle again, knowing that I have time on open road before I come upon slower traffic. Sometimes I just don't have the aggressive attitude needed to pass ten cars, plus, it's safer. (Nigel calls it playing "catch up".)

You'll reach the summit of San Marcos Pass about seven and a half miles into your trip. After topping out at 2,224 feet, Highway 154 becomes a downhill jaunt, with a steep seven percent grade for four miles. It's straighter than you'd expect for a run down the backside of a mountain, yet it's a course that's still fun and diverse enough to satisfy most enthusiasts. Also, to make passing safe and easy on this downward swing, you'll have two lanes on your side of the highway for several miles.

As you continue your descent from the upper reaches of this highway, you'll have fantastic views of the Santa Ynez Mountains as they gracefully embrace a lovely valley. A strategically placed vantage point at about the ten mile mark allows an unimpeded view of this attractive sight.

At about the 12 mile mark, the road bottoms out into a long valley, causing this highway's contours to straighten considerably. Surrounded by rolling foothills dotted with oak trees, the road begins to take on the atmosphere of a country lane. If the calendar has moved much into spring, you're likely to see the foothills draped in a golden blond color, though soon after the first fall rains the landscape turns a lush shade of green.

Once on the valley floor you'll soon find Lake Cachuma making an appearance on your right-hand side. Though Highway 154 doesn't run right up along its shore, glimpses are available from the highway. For better views of the lake, there's a clearly marked turnoff at about 18 miles. There you'll also find crude portable toilets on a paved lot. I guess you could picnic at this rest stop but more scenic places await the patient traveler along Highway 154.

As San Marcos Pass continues past Lake Cachuma on its northwesterly course, you'll encounter smooth, easy to handle curves—though long, hilly straights continue to dominate. This layout gives the motorist plenty of freedom to enjoy the lovely scenery that fills this valley. Several horse farms—complete with rolling green meadows full of galloping, prancing horses—make this stretch of highway a memorable one. If Ferrari ever decided to film a commercial in America, this is surely where they'd do it.

As you near the end of this trek, you'll be brought back to reality with the sighting of several housing tracks on the outskirts of the town of Los Olivos. The last couple of miles are an up-and-over run through rolling foothills—bringing a curvy bend to the road that you haven't seen since before Lake Cachuma.

Highway 154 concludes at a stop sign at the 32 mile mark. It's here that you meet up again with Highway 101. Your options are to head south towards Buellton, or north towards Santa Maria, Or, if you've got the time, turn around and head back along the path just traveled.

More than once I've been passed by autos doing over 130 mph on the longer straights that cut through this valley. In particular, I remember a silver Porsche 928S4 passing me one hot summer day at what seemed like almost double my speed (no small feat, folks). Many enthusiasts from the Santa Barbara area use this road's magnificient matchup of silky smooth straights and winding mountain passages to explore their vehicle's limits—so you're sure to rub shoulders with plenty of high performance vehicles on San Marcos Pass.

Another plus is that patrol—courtesy of the CHP—is usually light on Highway 154. Add a road surface in uniformly good condition and you begin to understand why this road is such fun to drive and ride.

If you normally travel north on Highway 101, you'll save about 13 miles by heading inland on San Marcos Pass. Besides being a short-cut, you'll also bypass some of the heavier traffic on Highway 101, especially near Gaviota. Plus, you'll miss one of the more heavily patrolled stretches of Highway 101. Maybe it's the CHP office just west of Goleta; I always seem to see more than my share of black-and-whites on Highway 101 between Santa Barbara and Gaviota. In addition, one of the CHP spotter planes frequently sees action on the stretch of Highway 101 north of Santa Barbara.

But, on the other hand, by taking the more adventurous Highway 154, you'll be skipping one of the most appealing stretches of Highway 101. From about six miles past Goleta (heading north), you'll find Highway 101 blessed with an abundance of great scenery. For a good 20 miles it runs like a shoeless child in summer, frolicking along the edges of the Pacific Ocean. Wildflowers spring up all along the road, adding even more color to this jaunt, It's easily one of the prettiest stretches in California.

For the enthusiast, Highway 101 is good, no-nonsense, four-lane Interstate driving, much of it ideal for higher speeds. Over the years I've split my time about evenly between Highway 101 and 154.

Between the two roads, I derive the most driving pleasure from San Marcos Pass. But sometimes the thought of Highway 101's ocean views steer me west, especially if it's near sunset. But which ever way you go, you're sure to find a path of pleasure.

And Nigel?

Oh, he's still in the commodities business. Last I heard, he'd sold the Ferrari and gotten his hands on a U.S. spec Lamborghini Countach.

Man, imagine that, 12 churning cylinders—working like metallic sutures.

Ready to close the wound at the turn of a key...

Highway 178

Direction: East.
Distance: About 85 miles.
Driving time: Two to four hours.
Congestion: Light to medium. Often heavy around lake.
Road condition: Very good.
Patrol: Light.

Now this is a road with variety. Its repertoire includes a feast of visual treats: a shaded river, jagged mountain peaks, lovely forest and grazing lands, and even a touch of sun-baked desert. But what really grabs this road big points is that it offers just as much variety in the driving and riding departments as it does in providing a kaleidoscope of landscapes.

Starting in the southern end of the fertile San Joaquin Valley, Highway 178 makes an inauspicious start passing through Bakersfield. The first six miles of Highway 178 can best be described as boring and non-descript (and that's being nice). Coursing through town—looking remarkably like a freeway at times—our road takes less than ten minutes to get us to the eastern outskirts of Bakersfield.

About seven miles out, things begin to look up as you travel on a long straight over a summit that leads to a picturesque valley. The road remains a gentle path, with long straights connected to easy, low-g sweepers. But driving gets more interesting as Highway 178 aims for the southern Sierra Nevada mountains that jut out from the horizon. Moving closer to the base of these mountains, the terrain begins to quickly change with chunks of granite appearing like some sort of roadside welcoming committee.

At about the 15 mile mark, you'll hit the first hot stretch of road. Beginning with a flurry of road signs cautioning that a change is due, Highway 178 tiptoes into the mountains on a great series of esses. The road packs tight against solid walls of granite; fat fingers of rock pushing out towards the road off on your right side. As the pavement slashes through the gaps carved out by a once mighty river, you'll be greeted by freshly paved asphalt that will whisk travelers along 15 miles of great curves and esses. Moving in a northeasterly direction, the highway begins rising slowly, narrowing some as it continues its dips and twists.

These bustling 15 miles of fun driving and riding also provide big rewards in the scenery department with the beautiful Kern River lying just a few feet from the road. Its riverbed is full of giant stones that act like speakers, amplifying the water's relentless and wonderful sounding assault upon the rocks. Various turnoffs along this road make it easy to get close to this river, though most of the turnouts can accommodate only two or three vehicles. (Motorcyclists, as usual, will have no problem finding a place to park.) The Kern River is a popular spot for rafting and picnicking. All in all, this is a fine stretch of road, full of interesting bends and eye-pleasing scenery.

At about the same time you hit the first fun stretch of Highway 178, you'll also enter Sequoia National Forest. Our highway runs within its confines for a pretty 20 miles. It's lovely—though Highway 178 misses several of the more scenic sections of this fine national park. Only signs posted along the road give away the boundaries of this beautiful forest.

After traveling a little over 30 miles, Highway 178 changes significantly. Gaining a lane, you'll feel like you're on a freeway instead of a back road. This stretch of Highway 178 has pavement as smooth as glass. Full of wide, low-g sweepers, it'll whet your appetite for higher speeds—speeds unobtainable while passing through the tight course found earlier on Highway 178. One clue is the number of 55 mph curve speed signs posted on this section. Experience tells me that on this well engineered stretch of highway, a lot of people would have to hit the brakes hard to get down to the double nickel speed limit. You'll continue rising as the surrounding mountain tops creep towards the road, making the passage feel a bit snug. About 40 miles out, the mountains finally give way to a long valley that's home for Lake Isabella.

Lake Isabella, a man-made lake, was created in 1953. This rather ordinary-looking, L-shaped lake will be to your left as you venture east on Highway 178. I find the miles along this lake pleasant, though certainly not spectacular. Thankfully, Highway 178 dishes up plenty of interesting road, utilizing short straights and medium to medium-tight curves to nip through the foothills surrounding Lake Isabella.

As I mentioned, this lake's shoreline adds little to the scenery. Paradise Campground, located on the south shore, seems typical. It looks like someone went crazy with a cement truck in the dark—indiscriminately pouring concrete along a potentially attractive shoreline. And there it sits looking barren and desolate; waiting for the seasonal onslaught of the camper and trailer set—folks evidently more than willing to put up with places like this. I often wonder, if someone considers staying here a vacation, just what does where they come from look like?

On this highway you'll pass through several small communities, including Lake Isabella, Mountain Mesa, and South Lake. All seem non-descript, marred by tacky real estate joints hawking acreage and lots. I often joke that it's towns like these that give the open road such a good reputation.

Next, you'll drive through the small community of Bella Vista, usually an uneventful experience. Be careful during heavy rains, as this stretch of road can quickly flood. As you continue on, you'll pass through a small valley where ranches mingle uneasily with mobile homes.

As you leave Lake Isabella behind, you'll begin to climb again. Look back towards the west and you'll be treated to several lovely panoramas of the lake. At this point, Highway 178 offers little that's difficult to handle, making it easy to enjoy the scenery. Plenty of half mile straights and slow bends fill the stretch of road between Lake Isabella and the community of Onyx. Much of the land on this stretch is used for grazing cattle, sheep, and horses. Additional ground is taken for farming, though the acreage set aside here is miniscule when compared to the big co-op farms that fill San Joaquin Valley—where we began our journey.

One of my favorite places on Highway 178 is the Onyx General Store, lying about 60 miles into our journey. This establishment, built in 1880, is a good place to stop and enjoy a cold drink. In the summer months, it can be an especially welcome oasis as valley temperatures often hit the 90's. This historic landmark, painted a traditional white, is fronted by a wooden porch offering plenty of room to rest for a while.

It was here one spring day that I met an old, grizzled American Indian named Wolf. His coarse laugh gave away a grin missing more than a few front teeth. A slow but steady gait—revealing just a hint of limp—did little to betray his age. We sat for hours, talking in the shade of the trees that hung over the store's long porch.

I asked Wolf what he did and he answered sternly, "Break colts."

I asked him if it was hard work, and with a hearty laugh, he said, "I got scars on my goddamn belly, my goddamn back, my goddamn legs, my goddamn head, yeah, it's kinda tough, ya gotta watch 'em, can't let 'em turn on ya."

Please understand, even though Wolf used what might be considered a liberal amount of obscenities, it was actually his way of punctuating what he felt were important points in the conversation. I listened to this tough, old Indian talk about everything from the big flood back in '66 to where his little farm was ("Goddamn flood, goddamn farm, goddamn tractor...").

As the afternoon slipped by, Wolf tackled every topic—whether it be indoor plumbing or television—with a bizarre blend of ancient Indian sayings and quasi-eastern religion. Stop by the Onyx General Store, it's sure to do ya' good.

Continuing on past Onyx, wide curves and fast straights make the road interesting for another six or so miles. After that, driving quickly gets hectic as the path begins to sneak upward through mountain passes.

The landscape also changes upon leaving Onyx, gradually turning arid and desert-like. Beginning with the first sighting of Joshua trees on Highway 178, our trail becomes increasingly remote and isolated. But you'll hardly have time to notice since another slice of exciting road soon asks for all of your attention; taking shape as a series of exciting lefts and rights about a half dozen miles past Onyx. Straight road then reintroduces itself, only to be replaced by the next sporting chunk noted below.

Surely the best stretch east of Onyx lies just past a 25 mph curve speed sign—out around the 70 mile mark. It acts as a starting flag for ten miles of rip-roaring driving on road that's usually free of traffic. This swirling, upward path escalates through the scenic high desert foothills, giving you a ride that's fast and fun with more changes in direction than a ride on one of Wolf's unbroken colts. Full of beautifully banked curves, it's here that the fun begins again in earnest. Adding to this road's playful mood are several wide horseshoe bends—allowing an enjoyable look back at the pavement just challenged.

Coursing through the high desert's chaparral-covered foothills and mountains, enthusiasts will have a hard time keeping the speed down. Several tight (20 mph) turns make it mandatory that you take it slow in a few spots. Thankfully, the last time I drove through here, all the tight corners were well marked with curve speed advisory information.

As you hurtle off of Walker Pass, Highway 178 casts you towards the hot desert floor. This section will propel most vehicles into the 70's and 80's without much effort on your part. The slightest movement of the throttle towards the firewall will ensure a visit to triple-digit territory on these last seven miles of our trip.

In less than a hundred miles, Highway 178 has taken you from the forest of Sequoia along a winding river road, through massive stone corridors, towards a finish on a desolate desert highway where pine and cactus grow side by side.

A stop sign at a T-shaped intersection with Highway 14 marks the end of this journey. A left turn onto Highway 14 takes you to well-known Highway 395, seven miles north. Head south on Highway

14 and you'll travel over 120 miles before reaching the outskirts of Los Angeles.

I've never seen a CHP vehicle on the desert side of Walker Pass, though I'm sure they get out there on a regular basis. The CHP seems almost as scarce on the rest of Highway 178. And that's good, because Highway 178 is in great condition, making it a joy to run at higher speeds.

Highway 178 offers the enthusiast a variety of surfaces and scenery that reflect California's true beauty like few highways can. And though it might not be the handiest road in California, its constant diversity make it a natural choice for this guide.

CHAPTER 5

BEST
ROADS
OF
NORTHERN
CALIFORNIA

Highway 1 (North route)

Direction: North.
Distance: About 205 miles.
Driving time: From five to eight hours.
Congestion: Usually light, occasionally moderate to heavy.
Road condition: Good, except for the first 30 miles.
Patrol: Light to moderate.

Many of the driving enthusiasts living in the Bay Area are familiar with this jewel of a road. Beginning just north of the Golden Gate Bridge, Highway 1 takes you on a five to eight hour jaunt along the rugged Northern California coast. This impressive passage offers spectacular scenery and plenty of satisfaction for the driving and riding enthusiast. It's the kind of journey that could just as easily take a week as a day.

Those lucky enough to start their journey in San Francisco should head north on Highway 101—across the famous Golden Gate Bridge. Several miles later you'll find the clearly marked exit for Stinson Beach and Highway 1.

The first few miles run through an uninspiring commercial district followed by a short, but pleasant drive on a winding residential road. Leave this stretch, and you'll run on the rim of a canyon that opens to beautiful views of Muir Beach and the indelible Pacific Ocean. A little green farm tucked into the valley on your left-hand side is Green Gulch Farm, a Zen retreat.

This little canyon path squiggles downwards towards the beach, then flattens considerably. Those who love to take canyons in the higher rpm's will be in for a treat. But if you plan on driving this stretch aggressively, you'd better forget about enjoying the scenery as this piece of road can be a handful.

At about the six mile mark. you'll need to make two left turns to stay on Highway 1—both clearly posted. You'll head briefly upwards through a sparse, yet beautiful residential area full of expensive homes perched on top of hills that spread in all directions. Upon leaving the "neighborhood", Highway 1 clings to the rocky cliffs as it now begins to run parallel with the coast, providing the traveler with unimpeded views of the craggy California shoreline.

The next stretch of fun road comes just past Stinson Beach,

beginning near Bolinas Lagoon. Often with ducks as roadside companions, you'll drive a stretch of highway that's close to perfect. With its winning combination of smooth lefts and rights, fun was what they obviously had in mind when they built this chunk of Highway 1. Along with the twists, you'll also find less demanding stretches, allowing you to enjoy the lovely farms and ranches that are spread along this road.

The miles along Bolinas Lagoon are easily one of the driving highlights of Highway 1. They're in beautiful shape and offer much driving and riding pleasure. And, if you leave town early enough, you'll encounter little traffic on this section even on the weekends.

A small grove of eucalyptus trees will mark yet another change in scenery and road surface on Highway 1. You'll leave the marshes and lagoons for a whirl through a long canyon. Highway 1 continues northward as a first class road, but rather than being tough on the limbs and brain, most of the turns are now smooth and gentle. You'll probably notice the thick forests of pine that lay off to your left at about the 20 mile mark. These belong to Point Reyes National Seashore.

The leg from Bolinas Lagoon to Olema is pleasant, if not spectacular road. Several stretches bound over little hills, allowing you the luxury of previewing the road ahead. Cattle often fill the landscape on this nine mile section of Highway 1. On occasion they get loose on the road, only missing a familiar orange tint to qualify as the largest slalom cones you've ever seen. Keep your eyes open.

Upon leaving the little community of Olema, you'll hit Point Reyes Station. To stay on Highway 1, watch for the right turn you'll need to make at the intersection where the Alliance gas station is located. Many people miss this turn because the road sign keeps getting stolen.

A couple of miles out of Point Reyes finds Highway 1 skirting along the southeastern edge of Tomales Bay. Before the path turns inland, this pretty bay will be your main source of scenery for about 12 miles. The road now consists of short straights connected to curves that lie in the medium-to-wide range. Occasionally, you'll encounter heavy traffic as you pass through Marshall, about halfway along Tomales Bay. But but one of the great things about this byway is that just down the road it always has something new for the enthusiast.

As you head northeast into Tomales, Highway 1 once again cuts a course across small hills. And it's near here that you'll say goodbye to the ocean views for a while. Highway 1 makes up for the loss of scenery with a mile of slalom-like pavement poured along Keys Creek that's guaranteed to lift your spirits.

Exiting Tomales brings a long straight that could easily grace the cover of any travel magazine. With eucalyptus groves framing golden meadows, you'll not forget this stunning sight for a long time to come. This solitary stretch of Highway 1 embodies much of what makes the open road such a wonderful experience.

At about the 50 mile mark, you'll make a left at the stop sign and head towards Bodega Bay. Traveling in a westerly direction, Highway 1 continues to traverse grasslands and farmlands so pretty, that roaming this road feels more like a privilege than a right.

Unfortunately, you'll begin to pick up traffic as you head towards Bodega Bay. But once you get through this busy little fishing and resort town, you'll again be rewarded with terrific road. After your brief inland travels, the whitecapped waves of the Pacific Ocean become visible again just short of Bodega Bay

As you head north out of this seaside resort, you'll have plenty of turnouts for resting or photo taking on the ocean side of Highway 1. Another plus is the nice series of curves and turns comprising a nifty stretch of Highway 1 that's just past Bodega Bay—but watch out for the campers and inattentive tourists pulling out from the many cliffside vista points. Logging trucks, slogging up and down this highway, can also be a major distraction from the fun at hand; though you're more likely to find the big rigs on the second half of our excursion, and then, mainly on weekdays.

The small town of Jenner will greet you at about the 70 mile mark. After leaving this community, you'll encounter fewer straights and tighter curves. Highway 1 again straightens out a couple of miles south of Stewarts Point, just short of the 100 mile mark. Some of the best scenery on Highway 1 lies between Jenner and Stewarts Point, full of beautiful ocean views and lush pine forests that, at times, seem to swallow this two-lane highway into a cool darkness.

As you pass the 100 mile mark, you'll be running high above the ocean using u-shaped excursions as the road skirts along the outlines of the numerous small inlets Highway 1 is built along. Most of these inlets run a mile or so and must be done at a reduced speed.

North of Point Arena, you'll find cows and sheep grazing on grassy plateaus called marine terraces. Much of Highway 1 is built on these geological wonders. The community of Mendocino rests upon one. You can usually tell you're on a marine terrace by looking for land that slopes gently down toward the sea—often ending as the jagged edges of ocean cliffs. They're actually old beaches slowly planed over millions of years by the action of waves, only then to be lifted above sea level by the slow uplifting of the ancient Coast Range. In this region you'll often see these terraces used for farming.

While we're on the subject of geology, I would be amiss if I didn't mention that this section of California is what geologists refer to as the Salinian block. Over a period of millions of years it's moved about 350 miles north, along the San Andreas Fault. This movement has created more than its share of earthquakes, big and small. I always get a funny feeling while driving this section of Highway 1 knowing that eons ago this area was sitting hundreds of miles south of here.

North of the little town of Manchester you'll encounter straights of sufficient length to use higher gears. Friendly locals tell me that triple digit speeds are not unheard of on this stretch. The ocean now will rarely be more than a mile away. Looking at my log book, the stretch between Manchester and Elk elicited this entry, "Drive a half mile straight; then a posted 30 mph turn; followed by two posted 50 mph turns; and finally a quarter mile straight where speeds can approach 90 mph; heading back into quick left and right turns".

Whew!

It's a great stretch to work on your heel-and-toe technique, with a lot of shifting required to keep the torque in a user-friendly range. Typical (typical!) scenery includes panoramic ocean views on your left and serene grazing lands off to your right.

At the intersection of Highways 1 and 128, traffic usually picks up considerably. This intersection lies about ten miles south of Mendocino. The ride into this unique Northern California town will be governed by the level of traffic, but it's unlikely that you'll be anywhere near your upper limits as you roll into Mendocino.

Mendocino is as close as many Californians get to New England. Full of quaint cottages and Victorian homes, this town obviously missed out on much of the Mexican influence. It's become an artist colony, which means all the restaurants and bed and breakfasts can charge more.

Many of you may want to consider ending your journey in Mendocino, maybe spending the night; you could even turn around and head back towards the Bay Area. After all, up to this point, you've traveled 150 miles of great road. In addition, you'll continue to find the road congested on the leg into Fort Bragg, about 11 miles north of Mendocino. And, for a time, Highway 1 loses that back road feel that makes it such a joy to drive and ride. Now it feels more like Highway 101, the four-laner sitting to the east. But, if you're willing, and not too fatigued, there's still plenty of good road ahead.

Those hearty souls continuing on will have their patience rewarded a few miles out of Fort Bragg. First, traffic thins quickly, and when looking at a map of this region it's easy to understand why. Few people use this part of Highway 1 for travel since it leads to Leggett (not exactly a big destination for the young and restless). Plus, most locals head south to Highway 20 to connect with Highway 101.

Continuing on north of Fort Bragg, you'll ride along with the ocean on a well maintained road that combines high speed straights with a wide assortment of pleasant curves. This stretch is sure to ease the pain inflicted by the slow moving Mendocino-Fort Bragg leg of our trip.

The last 20 mile segment takes an easterly course, moving inland through what are known as second growth forests. Though most of the original redwoods that grew here are now gone, you'll find the newest growth of trees attractive and peaceful, as if the current woods were the original tenants. This road winds slowly (30 mph is tops in most places) through heavily forested ridges and ravines. There are no communities to speak of along this road, just some nice spots to stop and enjoy the solitude.

For anyone suffering from fatigue, these final miles can be a tortuous drive. But those well rested will find it a fun, tightly wound path through most pleasant surroundings. Use good judgement before taking on the additional hour or so (each way) that's needed to safely drive these last few miles. Traffic will be very light most times, all the way to the junction of Highway 101—our journey's end.

One thing I really like about this 200 mile piece of Highway 1 is that there are no big, flashy "tourist attractions" along its path. With Mendocino as its focal point, this Northern California trail has a rare peacefulness along its environs that most travelers will find inviting. Almost hamlet-like in nature, the small, quaint villages spread along this highway only add to its charm. Highway 1 is also blessed with an abundance of interesting places to stay and eat. Yet, for me, its true strength lies in the long stretches of road that hold little evidence of civilization.

This is a well maintained highway, but not one without problems. During the rainy season, mud slides can frequently occur in the first 30 or so miles. Before leaving, you might want to call the California Highway Information Network (CHIN) phone number for an update on road conditions for this area (see the Appendix for phone numbers). You're also likely to encounter the California Highway Patrol at least once—so keep an eye out. Also plan on occasionally sharing the road with the brown and white truck-like vehicles of the county sheriff. And though I've never encountered any speed traps along this road, the local sheriffs around here are rumored to get a bit aggressive at times.

In an odd way, I worry about this highway. Much of its southern portion closely traces the famous San Andreas fault, source of the deadly 1906 San Francisco earthquake. In fact, many geologists predict that communities like Stinson Beach will simply cease to exist when the "big one" finally hits because they are built on what experts call a sandspit—a very unstable foundation to put a building on. Thankfully, the San Andreas fault leaves California about 12 miles north of Point Arena, near the mouth of Alder Creek. From there it continues to run parallel to our coastline for quite a few miles before disappearing altogether.

Famous faults, ocean vistas, eccentric little towns, so much is waiting for you on this illustrious road. To me, it's just another feather in the cap of a road that's found its way onto a lot of the pages of this guide, California's incomparable Highway 1.

Highway 35

Direction: North.
Distance: 26 miles.
Driving time: About an hour.
Congestion: Light to moderate.
Road condition: Good.
Patrol: Light.

Though only 26 miles long, Highway 35 is surprisingly diverse in its content and texture. Built to skirt along the top of California's last mountain range before the Pacific Ocean, it affords views of not only the land running towards the ocean, but also the broad valley lying to the east that plays host to San Jose, San Mateo, and others. Plus, several park and game preserves lying along Highway 35 translate into beautiful tree lined passages, cooled and darkened by thick forests of pine and redwood.

Many people in the Bay Area will find this an easy road to reach. The northern terminus of Highway 35 is only about 15 miles south of San Francisco. People living in the "Silicon Valley" have an even shorter drive on Highway 9, through the community of Saratoga.

Highway 35 is an everchanging road that's often unpredictable. One minute it's an easy, smooth tour on half mile straights; the next minute it feels like a paved motorcross course—full of tight esses—forcing you to reach for all the skill you have to stay on top of this two-lane.

We begin our trek on Highway 35 at the four-way stop where Highways 9 and 35 meet. To get there you've probably already done some significant climbing, with the elevation at Saratoga Gap, a few miles west of our start, sitting at 2,634 feet.

Beginning with a mixture of short straights and medium curves, the first few miles act more like an easy warmup than a real workout. There's certainly nothing difficult about the first two miles. But after that, Highway 35 begins to turn out snippets of twisty road—usually in little quarter mile chunks. Hilly along its entire path, Highway 35 can rise and fall in big movements, while at other times, the hills are barely perceptible.

An endless series of hills, valleys, and mountains off to your left make up the first five miles of scenery. During the long California

114

summers, they're bathed in a warm blond, while the rainy season carpets this landscape in a velvet-like green. Unfortunately, any views of the heavily populated valley to your right will be shrouded by trees and forests for about the first seven miles.

I love this road early in the morning, when traffic is light, though that sometimes means traveling through fog to reach this lofty road. But once on Highway 35, you'll often be high enough to look down on the long valley to the east—often appearing as a bed of billowy cotton balls if the fog has yet to lift. A perfectly placed vista point at about seven miles allows an unimpeded view of this valley.

Exploring the first half of Highway 35 finds a potpourri of twists, curves, and straights that defy description. Rising and falling along the mountain tops, every curve exposes you to a different camber and bend. My only regret about this road is that the best stretches come in spurts—lasting only for a mile or two each time—always leaving the enthusiast in me longing for one more twist, one more fast curl.

The first section ends at the intersection of Highway 35 and 84. This also happens to be the home of the infamous Alice's Restaurant. This well-known establishment is a favorite meeting spot for Bay Area motorcyclists; their two-wheeled vehicles easily outnumbering the few cars that manage to squeeze into the parking area out front.

Many people have a fondness for this place that might be difficult to comprehend upon your first visit to Alice's. First, is the food. To say that Alice's is not exactly a gourmet restaurant is an understatement. But if your looking for great food, you've come to the wrong place. (Actually, if you're looking for just average food, you've *still* come to the wrong place.) Food is not what brings people to Alice's. This is hallowed ground, a meeting point, a piece of history. Somehow all the idiosyncrasies give this crazy joint a disposition that makes people feel most welcome. Coming to Alice's is a lot like going home to long lost (but not greatly loved) relatives; you feel good being there, but you feel even better knowing your stay will be brief.

You see, bad food, smoking waitresses, outdoor toilets, brightly colored mix-and-matched vinyl furniture—none of it matters. This eclectic place is judged by a different set of standards. And it has to be, as Alice's would have a tough time existing elsewhere. But, sitting on its mountain top, miles from the competition, holding a place in many people's hearts—it survives above the whims of the fickle bunch living in the valley below.

The second half of this road is geared to aggressive driving and riding. Plenty of medium to medium-tight curves connected to short straights make up this portion of Highway 35. Snaking along through the mountains, it gets a little bumpy in places, but overall the asphalt is in good shape. Potential hazards include a rock slide warning (well marked) around the 18 mile mark—but it's nothing too serious.

My favorite piece of Highway 35 is the five mile stretch heading north after leaving Alice's Restaurant. It's full of delightful surprises, leading you left, right, up, down, and then every once in a while spitting you out on a short straight—barely giving you enough time to catch your breath before the next twist in the road.

After that, the last few miles take you quickly downward using a tightly wound path that's nearly as much fun. You'll finish up at the junction of Highways 35 and 92. Make a left, and five miles later you'll reach Highway 1 and the Pacific Ocean. Turn right, and you'll head towards Interstate 280 and civilization.

Highway 35 is complimented by lovely forests of pine and redwood along much of its path, but they are especially thick on the second half. Often growing right up to the road, these stands of trees create a serene atmosphere that the weary traveler will find soothing. Several more great views wait for you on this path. The best-of-the-rest includes a heart-stopping view (around 22 miles out) of a lovely valley, but be on the lookout as it passes quickly.

As you drive Highway 35, be on guard for bicyclists. With no bicycle lane available, they often drift out into the middle of the road. This is also a favorite road for Bay Area motorcyclists. But, with the motorized two-wheelers, you'll often have the opposite problem. I'm always joined on this road by sleek sport bikes; their owners, decked out in brightly colored racing leathers, zooming by me, nailing each cut of the road like there's no tomorrow. Sunday mornings on this road can get congested, and depending on your attitude, is either the worst or best time to be on Highway 35. Surprisingly, Saturday morning can be less hectic, and is usually my favorite time to take this road.

Highway 35 is also one of those trails that's almost as fun to get to as it is to drive. From San Francisco, I suggest you take Highway 1 south to Highway 84—an exciting road in its own right. Take Highway 84 east and you'll find increasingly tighter turf, with the long even straights of the first half of Highway 84 giving way to tight, hilly road as you near the junction of Highways 84 and 35 (home of Alice's Restaurant). The last couple of miles of Highway 84 have some shoddy patch work, so be careful. Motorcyclists should use utmost care, as a few of the lumps and bumps are severe. Patrol seems light on Highway 35, though I wouldn't take this as gospel. Popularity has a way of spoiling a road, enticing all kinds of folks to come out—including the local authorities.

Those living in the San Jose area and Oakland farther north, have

Highway 9 as their corridor to Highway 35. Highway 9 offers up fun, twisty road—though it's a bit narrow in places. Its lovely wooded scenery acts as a precursor to what lies ahead on our featured road. Highway 9 can get congested, especially on the weekends. It has a limited speed limit that the locals tells me is often enforced with radar, though I've never seen it. It's about seven miles from downtown Saratoga to the start of Highway 35.

Highway 35 is an elusive road. Usually a good road will alternate fun groundwork with stretches of pleasant scenery. But this highway has a tendency to be more complex—more difficult to catagorize. Full of surprises in a most pleasant way, it's easy to see why this spirited road is a favorite with so many of California's driving and riding enthusiasts.

Highway 36

Direction: West.
Distance: About 140 miles.
Driving time: From four to six hours.
Congestion: Light.
Road condition: Good.
Patrol: Light.

Looking at a map of upper Northern California, you see two highways linking Interstate 5 with Highway 101 to the west. They are Highway 299 (also in this guide) and Highway 36. On comparing the two, Highway 299 is the quickest route. It's a modern well maintained highway with great, if not spectacular, scenery.

In contrast, Highway 36, starting about 30 miles south of Highway 299, is an older road with more character. It's a lightly traveled path with that wonderful back road feel to it. You should know that it's not in the greatest condition in places—and even narrows to one lane on occasion. But, if you're willing to put up with this road's cantankerous ways, you'll discover a delicious blend of scenery ranging from towering redwood groves to oak-studded foothills. And like any good road, it boasts stretches of fabulously fun road for the enthusiast. If you have the time and a sense of adventure, then Highway 36 is for you.

Starting out at Red Bluff, a small community off of Interstate 5, Highway 36 springs to life just beyond the railroad tracks north of town. One reason why I like this road so much is because the best chunk of driving waits at the start. From just out of Red Bluff—from the railroad tracks on—Highway 36 lays down 30 miles of some of the best road California has to offer. This trail of asphalt comes complete with a rambunctious collection of curves, bends, and twists that combine forces to toss cars around like confetti at a party.

Another delightful aspect of driving the first 30 miles of Highway 36 is the tricky hills that, at high speeds, can instantly enlist you as a member of the airborne corps. A few of these hills corrupt gravity so abruptly that drivers and riders taking this trail at a quick pace will feel like they're on some sort of kamikaze training course. This devious back road snaps and crackles, and to the enthusiast it represents an irresistible challenge.

As you wrestle with this road, you'll spend much of your time traveling through scenic foothills dotted with stately groves of oaks. You'll see both live oak and blue oak on this stretch. (The blue oak is distinguished by little clumpy things in its upper branches; trust me, you'll know it when you see it.) And by the ten mile mark, you'll have lost sight of civilization, increasing this road's sense of adventurousness as you continue to venture westward into unchartered territory.

Traffic is extremely light on Highway 36, with only an occasional pickup truck interrupting your line of vision. The road is in good condition except for a few minor bumps and lumps that shouldn't cause much of a problem to well suspended vehicles. Plus, additional curve speed signs were finally installed in 1986, providing drivers with more information.

The first 30 miles also happen to be squirrel country, so keep an eye out for these permanent roadside residents. On occasion, you'll come over a rise and see one of these guys standing still in the middle of the road. Slow down, as all they're trying to do is get a bearing on your vehicle. You're not dealing with the brightest animals, so give them a second or two to figure out what's going on. Once they sense the danger they'll quickly scamper off of the road.

From the 30 mile mark to Plantina, a distance of about 15 miles, Highway 36 begins to straighten itself out, leaving behind the curves and sways for a chance to take on higher speeds. This 15 mile section is marked by quarter to half mile straights pieced together with easy, low-g sweepers.

In all, there are about ten small towns along our route. As you drive through each, you'll notice that they all seem to have two things in common: a couple of gas pumps and a small general or convenience store. Travelers will find plenty of goodies to eat and drink at each town's small store. Gas prices are usually exorbitant in these tiny hamlets so try to remember to gas up in Red Bluff before beginning your trek.

Each community along Highway 36 has its own subtle character, though it's often illusive to those just passing through. You can't help but wonder how these people ended up living out here. By asking politely, you're likely to be treated to a fascinating story sprinkled with the history of the region and the families who settled it.

After Platina, Highway 36 changes as you abandon the foothills and begin an upward path into a more mountainous forested area. Just a few miles out of Platina you'll enter Shasta-Trinity National Forest. For a good 50 miles, your travels will be through this natural wonder. The numerous lovely mountains, valleys, and meadows that make up this forest will yield many pleasures and few disappointments.

A good portion of the pavement in Shasta-Trinity has been recently resurfaced. But I'm sad to report that there's a tendency on the small back roads to not spend the time and money to get all the loose gravel cleaned up. So if you've just had a new paint job you may want to travel at a slower pace on this stretch of Highway 36.

At about the 70 mile mark, you'll hit a *possible* rock slide area. Work done in 1986 has improved a five mile stretch that typically had rocks the size of basketballs resting in the road. But keep alert, as these problems have a way of cropping up again. For the most part, you'll enjoy your drive through this secluded forest; often so lightly traveled that you'll see leaves—undisturbed by the whirl of traffic—carpeting this lonely highway.

After passing through the town of Forest Glen (about 75 miles into our trip), Highway 36 makes another significant change. Signs shouting "WINDING ROAD NEXT 14 MILES" and "ROAD NARROWS" don't come close to preparing you for what's next. The first time you drive this you might wonder if you've made a wrong turn. Suddenly you're on a darkened single lane road with not a straight in sight. Top speed through these wiggles is about 30 mph. What makes it all worthwhile is the impressive scenery. Traveling along a road laced with forests deep in pine, you'll soon leave Shasta-Trinity and immediately enter Six Rivers National Forest. Here you'll discover even more stunning views, and for 25 miles this rollicking back road finds its way west using hairpin curves and corkscrews.

This stretch will make continuous demands on the driver and rider. My advice on driving this coiled path is to take it slow and easy and enjoy the scenery. It's very narrow in places and parts of this grandfatherly old road haven't seen a center line in years. You'll drive for what seems like miles before you'll see a straight longer than your car. This section might be an excellent time to pull over and rest or change drivers as you'll have plenty of shady turnouts to choose from.

Work will continue well in the late 1980's on resurfacing portions of Highway 36. In 1987, work was being completed on a stretch near the 90 mile mark. Construction in progress often translates into torn-up pavement—often making travel on dirt and gravel necessary. Last time through here, I was held up for about ten minutes while heavy construction equipment pounded away at a quickly disappearing road surface. Every year between April and September—weather permitting—the private company handling the construction chores will continue to work in an easterly direction until they reach the Mad River.

As you leave Six Rivers National Forest (just past Dinsmore) the road makes a rapid descent made up of two separate grades. The first, a nine percent grade, is at about the 100 mile marker. The second grade follows about four miles later with an even steeper decline of ten percent. This final descent continues for about three miles, bringing you into a picturesque valley containing the Van Duzen River, often seen flowing along the road throughout the year. By this time Highway 36 will have become an easier drive. Tight, winding road is transformed into wide, easy curves. Straights reappear, too, making the remaining road a more leisurely trek.

Bridgeville is the first town you'll find upon completing your descent. On the 20 miles between Bridgeville and Carlotta, you'll again encounter fast and fun road that's loaded with medium curves and straights long enough to allow time in the higher gears.

Near the end of our trip you'll drive through the small Grizzly Creek Redwoods State Park, a grove of lofty redwoods that create a cool, tunnel-like sanctuary for travelers. If you're able to pull over and stop for a moment you'll be treated to the wonderful sights and sounds that permeate this idyllic domain. In some places, the redwoods grow out to the edge of the road. Flanked by these majestic giants, you'll be amazed at how they managed to squeeze this little two-lane roadway through this redwood jungle. For me, this is the most beautiful and inspiring section of our featured road.

You'll close out your drive by running through a small and colorful valley embracing grazing lands and pastures. The last town on this journey is Hydesville. From there, you are less than three miles from Highway 101, the western terminus of Highway 36.

I love the variety this road offers in scenery, terrain, and pavement. Highway 36 running from foothills at the start, to mountain forest in the middle miles, and closing with a cruise through a towering redwood grove, has plenty to offer. This splendid path is sometimes demanding and certainly requires an adventurous attitude, but it pays back in wonderful memories sure to last a lifetime.

In winter, snow at the higher altitudes makes this trek enjoyable only during warm weather. Though rarely closed by snow, I don't recommend this rural path except in the best of weather. Summer is the best time to explore Highway 36—though it can get very hot in the Red Bluff area. It does cool down as you move into the higher elevations to the west. Again, encountering any kind of adverse conditions should be cause to reassess any journey on Highway 36.

There is one more reason why this highway is so special to me. It was on this roadway many years back that I saw my first doe. Maybe not a big deal until you think about how many miles of road you can travel plastered with deer signs, and yet never see one.

My first glimpse was of her standing in the middle of the narrow road, looking small and frail, as if her thin spidery legs could barely support her weight. Strands of sunlight pierced through the tall forest, catching her nutbrown coat, further highlighting this delicate animal. She was everything a beautiful animal should be. Graceful, elegant, natural, godly.

I vividly remember her eyes locking into mine, searching for the answer to whether I was friend or foe. For just a second I had this crazy idea that maybe she would somehow sense my wonderment, my curiosity, and fight the age-old instinct to survive instilled deep inside her. But the dash to freedom was as natural an act to her as breathing—and so she fled into the dense forest.

I pulled off the road, hoping to savor the moment, lock it safely away, deep inside—forever mine. Sheltered by towering redwoods that filtered out the remaining evening light, I sat there for a long time on that lovely highway, the quiet of that ancient forest slowly chipping away at my frustration. I remember thinking that it's the simple, spontaneous things that seem to fill us with the most precious of memories. Memories that help spin wonderful, personal visions that never fail to warm the heart. Images that work eloquently, like a well-crafted love song that goes unabashedly for the heartstrings with just the right words, the right music, the right rhythm. This was one of those moments. It was too good, and too short.

My ideas of what made a good road got a few jolts that summer evening. New ideas, having little to do with machines, metal, or speed. And ten years later, the thought of a young doe on a secluded highway still kindles inside me a belief that all living things are like kindred spirits, sharing an unabated passion for life. Indelibly equal, yet unique.

I guess that every once in a while, we get lucky and get to see, touch, or be touched by something of great beauty, something truly wondrous.

Thank you, you grand old highway. I'll be back.

Highway 89

Direction: North.
Distance: About 360 miles.
Driving time: Two to three days.
Congestion: Mostly light. Heavier around Lake Tahoe.
Road condition: Good to very good.
Patrol: Light to moderate.

Highway 89 is a joyous path chock-full of fascinating scenery, communities, and people. I've decided to include the entire length of Highway 89 in this guide since it's a consistently fun and interesting road experience. *Do not* try to do it all in one day as this is a highway that rewards patience. And for those that have the time to linger, Highway 89 can be a wonderful destination in itself.

Highway 89 is not an all-season road. Monitor Pass is closed much of the year due to snow. Some years the snow is so hesitant to melt that they're lucky to get it open by July 4th. But in most years it's open by late May or early June. In the fall, sometimes the first snow melts quickly—not always closing Monitor Pass. But usually the road becomes impassable within a few weeks of the first snow fall. Most years all you've got is a three to four month period in which to experience the joys of Highway 89's higher elevations.

We begin our journey with a well marked turn onto Highway 89 from Highway 395. Those traveling north on Highway 395 will enjoy the drive along pretty Lake Topaz as a prelude to the trip on Highway 89.

Highway 89 begins life as a free-spirited mountain road, full of great lefts and rights that exhort the enthusiast to spend time near his limits. As you head dramatically upwards, you'll climb over 3,000 feet on a brisk ten miles to Monitor Pass. This is just the first of many high altitude summits on Highway 89, with this initial one topping out at 8,314 feet.

On this first stretch, you'll find the asphalt in fine condition— and that's surprising if you have an inkling about how cold and moisture can shorten the life of any pavement. But the 22 miles of Highway 89 leading up to Markleeville have received a lot of attention, resulting in roadtop that's as smooth as a baby's bottom (and sometimes just as hilly).

After slashing through narrow rock canyons, the thick slabs of stone retreat, giving way to the first of many majestic views along Highway 89. If the sight of the beautiful and unspoiled Slinkard Valley unfurling in front of you doesn't make you tingle, then nothing will. If ever there was *big country,* this is it. You'll find it lathered in green year-round, making serious picture taking a high priority. Unfortunately, places to stop are rare the first few miles. Just be patient, as turnoffs become plentiful once off the valley floor.

Moving through the north end of Slinkard Valley, the road straightens considerably. A few well placed medium turns help keep the road interesting, but for the impatient driver, switchbacks and twistys wait just minutes down the way.

Continuing to climb, the road begins to move away from the broad valley. Highway 89 now streaks through lush mountain meadows contained by a wide variety of pine. This lovely scenery continues for miles and when it combines with the fresh scent of pine, you'll begin to wonder why you waited so long to seek out this blissful highway.

You'll reach Monitor Pass at about the ten mile mark. Highway 89 begins spiraling downwards from there and it's a fun drive on road in good condition. No tight hairpins here, just miles of engaging twists and dips running through mountain tops bridged by beautiful meadows. And even during the warm months you'll be able to find little dabs of snow dotting the mountain passes.

Next out of Highway 89's repertoire comes a priceless collection of fast canyon runs that, even at half speed, are capable of captivating the most serious of enthusiasts. Forget the scenery, these squiggles will require that your full attention be transferred to the pavement ahead.

At about the 17 mile mark, you'll need to make a right turn at the junction of Highways 4 and 89. Once again, brace yourself for plenty of elevation changes. The lovely Carson River makes its first appearance, adding scenic relief on the highway between the junction of Highway 4 and Markleeville.

The small mountain community of Markleeville is the first sign of civilization and sets about 22 miles into our trek. This lovely mountain retreat boasts a pleasant general store in the middle of town. And in the tradition of the best small town stores, its white paint makes a great backdrop for the American flag that proudly waves out front. Inside the traveler will find some of the friendliest people anywhere.

You're always welcome to sit on the front porch—if you don't mind sharing your bench with the life-size Indian gracing this store's frontage. You'll also find clean restrooms out back. If their prices seem a tad high, just remember that people up here only have three or four months each year to make most of their living.

As we move on, you'll find the six mile stretch between Markleeville and the junction of Highway 88 overflowing with splendid scenery. As you pass through scenic valleys and lush meadows, you'll be pleased to find fairly straight road, enabling you to soak up the fantastic views this passage affords.

The next six miles are traveled on Highway 88/89 combined. It continues to be easy, high speed road with wide sweepers connected to straights that typically run in the quarter to half mile range.

At around the 35 mile mark, make a right turn at Pickett Junction to stay on Highway 89. From there you'll start with a mile long straight built on a slight incline. Its course takes you through a peaceful slice on land known as Hope Valley.

The stretch between Hope Valley and the junction of Highway 50 is about 11 miles long. It holds several great downhill runs—all wide and well surfaced. You'll find it easy to significantly exceed the double nickel—if that's your mood. But mountains studded with pine, aspen, and white fir, combined with pretty streams running alongside the roads, will collar most travelers, making speed unimportant for a time.

After a right to stay on Highway 89, you'll have a 40 mph speed limit to adhere to. Soon you'll begin to leave the impressive scenery behind as the pavement drops you onto Highway 50, one of the main feeder roads into the Lake Tahoe area.

Unfortunately, traffic will thicken during your brief five mile excursion onto Highway 50, and congestion is exhibit number one in my case for labeling this chunk of road, "worst of trip". Also, the landscape is devoid of pleasant scenery, instead treating the traveler to a host of cheap looking motels competing with each other for the most garish signage. I think this section offers plenty of examples of what happens when money becomes more important than people, or the land. After five miles, you'll gladly say goodbye to Highway 50 as it heads northeast with a right turn—but lucky you, you'll drive straight through a clearly marked intersection towards better times.

As you pass through this busy intersection, travel will continue through a commercial district at reduced speeds. Watch out for the CHP on this stretch, as they often work in teams enforcing a 35 mph speed limit. It seems about 10 mph too slow to me, but with patrol high and better road just seconds ahead, you won't see me forcing the issue.

The 28 miles of Highway 89 running from Highway 50 to Tahoe City is a trail of contrasts. Now, don't get me wrong, for those who love beautiful scenery this piece of Highway 89 is sure to satisfy.

You'll encounter breathtaking cliffside views like the one overlooking Emerald Bay; its sparkling blue waters graced with enchanting Fannette Island, a delicate, yet rocky mass that pierces the lake's rippling surface.

In addition, you'll find miles of deep pine forests that can make motoring a relaxing experience. There's an ample supply of campgrounds and picnic spots for eating and resting. Add mountainsides that reveal the voluptuous homes of the rich and famous, and you've got a highway that has something for everyone.

Of course we can't forget to mention the star of this impressive show, the great, beautiful Lake Tahoe. This natural wonder, about 22 miles long by 12 miles wide, is the focal point for a region best known for its winter sports. But a slew of warm weather activities including fishing, hiking, and riding make this region a year-round playground. Jammed between two rugged mountain ranges, this exquisite area has more idyllic scenery than any one roll of film could ever handle. Luckily, Highway 89 provides plenty of turnouts for leisurely enjoying the kind of views for which the word "panoramic" must have been invented.

Much of your travel along the outline of Lake Tahoe is within the confines of Tahoe National Forest, a region comprising about 700,000 acres. Here you'll find a good choice of tourist attractions, including everything from a mansion that's a replica of a 1,200 year old Viking fortress, to the ranch where they filmed a portion of the old TV western, *Bonanza.*

But it probably comes as no surprise that the drawing power of all this beauty has created a few problems. Over the years, the shoreline has become increasingly populated as more homes, businesses and resorts crowd in. Add the ever present tourist population, and the result is a road that's often choked with traffic; plan on sharing this bit of heaven with a heap of other folks. Also, you'll find several little villages—surely comfy places during the winter—that without a foot of snow to cover everything, quickly lose their quaintness, leaving Highway 89, at times, looking slightly frayed around the edges.

But I have to admit, the 28 mile stretch coursing along Lake Tahoe is a great road. Its menu is loaded with esses, twists, and curls, all with the potential to make this some of the best miles along Highway 89. But it's unlikely that you'll be able to take these morsels at true speed—speed allowing an intimacy with a road's contours that comes only from an enthusiastic touch of the controls. Heck, sometimes traffic is so bad on this road that I never *reach* the speed limit. It's unfortunate, but the popularity of this road has turned it into a drive of compromises: world-class scenery and views—but you'll give up a drive with more potential for fun than a date with a beauty queen.

At Tahoe City, you'll make a left turn and begin heading west—leaving Lake Tahoe behind. There's often a crowd in Tahoe City during the summer since this is the favorite starting point for rafters using the Truckee River. Motoring out of Tahoe City will fill your sights with a trove of pleasant scenery, much of it provided by the Truckee River. At times this river is a blur of fast white water, while at other points its waters are hard pressed to reach your ankles. This tree-lined river, running less than a hundred miles, ends in Nevada at Pyramid Lake. It's a most welcome roadside companion on the 14 miles between Tahoe City and Truckee.

The road from Tahoe City to the town of Truckee is geared towards higher speeds. Much of this stretch is marked by straights connected to long, sweeping curves. I get passed all the time by cars and bikes doing 80-85 mph. But be on guard, this section hides more than one fiesty swerve, that, if you're not alert, will force you to engage in a few quick arm-twists to stay on course.

Traffic is usually moderate up to Truckee, which sits just past the 90 mile mark of our trek. At Truckee you'll get on Interstate 80 for an mile or so before reaching the point where Highway 89 starts up again as a two-laner.

Upon exiting I-80, you'll lose most traffic. Shooting down that first long straight you'll find it difficult to keep your speed reasonable, but try, eh? Continuing northward towards Randolph, the curves become tighter, though most remain in the medium range. More demanding road begins about 14 miles north of Truckee; the tighter curves on this sporting section are posted with speeds in the 40 mph range.

Just about anywhere you pull over on this highway north of Truckee you'll hear the soothing sound of running water, Cold Stream Creek and Little Truckee River provide aqua inspiration for the stretch from Truckee to Randolph. Nearing Randolph, you'll find the scenery changing from pine-topped mountains to small, wooded valleys.

Just past Randolph you'll need to make a left turn to stay on Highway 89. It's another "combo" road. Now this one isn't going to make much sense. The road signs read, "HIGHWAY 89 NORTH, HIGHWAY 49 SOUTH". Well, that's a bit misleading; you don't actually head south on Highway 49, or 89 in fact, instead, you head north on Highway 49. It's just that in the bigger scheme of things, Highway 49 generally heads south, except for an occasional excursion north, here and there. Got all that? Good.

The six miles running as a combined Highway 49/89 begin life on a lovely note by sweeping gracefully through a beautiful valley.

Though still relying on mostly straight pavement, this portion begins to sneak progressively tighter curls onto the pathway. In addition, a herd of rambunctious hills introduce themselves, helping Highway 89 make the slow transformation back to an untamed road course. The fun-to-drive quotient of this road continues to increase to near outrageous proportions.

At the junction of Highway 49 you'll need to make a right turn to stay on Highway 89—where more excitement awaits the enthusiast. (A left will send you speeding south on Highway 49). After making the right, the road begins to change. Immediately the road becomes, well, more *playful*. Starting with two miles of tight twistys sculpted out of a handful of nifty little hills, Highway 89, using six slick miles of pavement, rises up about 500 feet to reach a summit of 5,441 feet.

More pleasures are awaiting the enthusiast upon entering Plumas County and Plumas National Forest. About a mile over the county line you'll encounter a short slalom that's best enjoyed by those holding a nimble touch. You'll have a couple of surprisingly tight turns, but all are posted with curve speed advisory information. Actually there are several rambling, slalom-like runs plundering the landscape on the stretch between the junction of Highways 49 and 89 and Blairsden. Alas, I'm sorry to report that just south of Blairsden, at Graegle, you'll often find traffic picking up a bit.

The next leg begins at the junction of Highways 70 and 89. Running about 35 miles, it branches northwest to the community of Paxton—where Highway 89 finally solos for a few miles. Highway 70 aims southwest towards Highway 99, making its own spirited path, much of it influenced by the cut of the Feather River.

The first few miles out of Paxton are made up of typical Highway 89: third to a half mile straights connected to slow, easy curves—with an occasional twisty section thrown in for good measure. On the straights I've often seen speeds in the 80-90 mph range. Locals tell me that they've seen speeds well over 100 mph at the end of a few straights! As usual, hearty pine fringes the road as our highway's sights continue to be shuffled with an ever changing variety of small, but endearing meadows and valleys.

The next community Highway 89 greets is Quincy. Unfortunately, this city is pockmarked with urban sprawl. The worst is just over a summit, where the unsuspecting traveler is met with a seemingly endless haul of burger stands, car dealers, drug stores, and all the things a growing city somewhere along the line decides it needs.

Quincy's elevation is 3,429 feet—a drop of about one thousand feet since leaving Blairsden. Making a right turn upon leaving Quincy keeps you on Highway 89. As with most cities straddling a two-laner, you'll have reduced speed limits in town, mostly in the 25-40 mph range.

And as if urban blight and traffic isn't enough to test your motoring mettle. Quincy is also the home of a CHP office. You'll find them keeping a high profile on the section of Highway 89 that's combined with Highway 70. And with plenty of the fast moving Mustangs in their stable, you'd be wise to keep an eye out if your plans include substantially exceeding the posted speed limit. The county sheriff also works this area, but they usually stick close to town and are relatively harmless. The locals are easily identified in vehicles painted brown and white.

On the road between Quincy and Paxton, the best visual nook is just past Keddle. Watch off to your right for a deep gorge with a pretty river tickling its bottom. The river's banks will usually be thick with greenery, making for a colorful picture. Good news for the enthusiast: the road between Keddle and Paxton is brimming with great twists and switchbacks, frequently giving this section the characteristics of a curling mountain road.

The next portion of Highway 89 will take you to a meeting with Highway 36. The starting point of this leg is a right hand turn outside of Paxton. You'll have the scenic Feather River flowing to your right, where numerous mining camps flourished during the Gold Rush days. The opposite side of the bank usually scales upward, neatly blending steep, pine-laden mountains into its shallow banks. Access to this river's uncrowded banks is practically hassle free, with plenty of parking along the road.

As usual, any time a road faithfully follows the contours of a river's banks, the enthusiast is almost always guaranteed a satisfying ride. With medium to tight turns, these seven miles along the Feather River can be harrowing or breathtaking—depending on your approach. Warning: I often encounter the CHP on this stretch, especially near Crescent Mills, where the river run concludes.

On this section of Highway 89 the only community you'll pass through of any size is Greenville. Leaving this small town finds you heading westerly on road with a range of delightful curves and bends reaching across beautifully laid asphalt. Rising again, this time you'll gain about one thousand feet in less than ten miles.

The run from Canyon Dam, sitting about 185 miles into our trip, is dominated by scenic Lake Almanor. This man-made lake was created in 1917 to help produce hydroelectric power. You'll be near water level when you first spy this secluded body of water, so it won't have the visual impact of Lake Tahoe, but it's a pretty sight, nonetheless. (I hear the fishing is first class.)

One of the joys of traveling this section of Highway 89 is the anticipation of catching the initial glimpse of towering Lassen Peak. For many the first sighting is trailing out of a big right-sweeper, that

129

as it straightens out, aims you right at Lassen's snowy peak, lying about 20 miles to the north. (More on Lassen Peak later in this summary.)

The road from Canyon Dam to Highway 36 is laid with long straights that encourage near flat-out driving. Few people travel this stretch at anywhere near the 55 mph speed limit. (I suspect, those that do are probably on their way down to a full stop.)

Next, you'll make a left turn to stay on Highway 89, now combined with Highway 36. It's about 27 miles from this junction until you reach the south entrance of Lassen National Park. The road contains few surprises; consisting mainly of straights connected to uneventful wide turns. The scenery, as usual, is dominated by forests of pine. Lush meadows occasionally appear, acting like nature's version of breathing room in this often rocky locale.

About eight miles past the junction of Highways 89 and 32 sets picturesque Childs Meadows. Cradled by mountains, it functions much like an opening act to one of the most scenic shows on Highway 89. You'll scale over one thousand feet on this four mile stretch—reaching Morgan Summit at about the 220 mile mark. The elevation of this high point is over 5,700 feet. The road between Childs Meadow and Morgan Summit—though a steep trail at times—is a truly fun and inventive road, whisking travelers upwards wielding a potpourri of dips and twirls.

Next you'll make a right turn at the signs pointing to Lassen Volcanic National Park. You'll encounter four miles of above average road tinged with a couple of short stretches that border on exhilarating. With formidable Lassen Peak now making frequent appearances between the pinetops, you'll continue to be impressed with the bounty of unspoiled beauty surrounding Highway 89.

Arrival at the south entrance to Lassen Volcanic National Park is at just under the 230 mile mark. Many might be surprised that I've included a road through a national park in this guide. After all, they're usually full of cars, campers, bikers, and people, right? Well, it's odd, but I've never encountered anything that came close to being labeled a crowd. This might be the most underrated national parks in California; it certainly is one of the least utilized.

What surprises me most about the road running through Lassen is what a fine drive it is. But when you take stock of this highway's attributes, it's got everything a fun road should have: a wide range of nicely banked curves and turns, light traffic, and a surface that's in superb condition. Add the fact that I've never seen the speed limit enforced, and you have the makings of a great road.

But *please* be careful when driving in this park. This is not a race course—it's a beautiful wilderness area. Maximum speed is 45 mph and the slower you drive, the more you'll see along this park's 28 mile trail. I usually do a lot of leisurely sight-seeing the first half, followed by a bit more driving the second half.

Those arriving around 9 a.m. will be rewarded with a quiet, peaceful journey, one that imparts a feeling that this place is *your* personal wilderness compound. That's amazing because the road for the whole park doesn't even open until about June 15, compressing the annual summer tourist season into just a few warm months.

Closing dates for the park depend on the first heavy snow, but the folks at the entrance gates tell me late September is typical, though up here, snow in July and August in not unheard of.

Lassen Volcanic National Park is dominated by Lassen Peak which last erupted over 70 years ago. On your cruise through this park, you'll pass numerous pristine lakes with Lake Helen and Lake Manzanita two of the prettiest. With landscapes laden with serene meadows and creeks, this terrific expanse of wilderness can make anyone with even a smidgen of photographic ability look like an ace picture-taker. But serious photographers will regret not having a wide-angle lens as this is grand country, and it sits up high, like a final brilliant jewel on top of nature's regal crown.

The section of Highway 89 that runs through Lassen Volcanic National Park provides plenty of places to pull over and enjoy the views; or you can just play in the snow as patches of the white stuff are easy (too easy) to find, even during summer. Last time I was here I had a terrific snowball fight against a clan of friendly Aussies clad in the gaudiest shorts I'd ever seen. They turned out to be sore losers; mooning the volcano and anything else looking remotely important as they pulled away from the battlefield.

If you want a good guide for driving in the park, I suggest you purchase a small booklet called *Road Guide—Lassen Volcanic National Park*. It's a bargain at about two bucks and it's sold at the Lassen Chalet, where the traveler can also find food, restrooms, souvenirs, and additional information. Lassen Chalet is located just inside the southern entrance to the park.

Leaving the park behind at about the 255 mile mark, a right turn will keep you on course. Our road quickly gets back to its old tricks: nice straights mingling among easy curves; the surrounding mountains continuing their sentinel-like vigil over our tour. You'll travel 36 miles, mostly through scenic Lassen National Forest, before meeting up with the junction of Highway 299.

But before that junction, you'll have the chance to investigate several great spots along this stretch. The best lies along a piece of road that runs with the curves of Hat Creek. There you'll find at least one spot where you can park just feet from the shallow banks of this little creek. Usually no more than ten feet across and a foot deep, you'll find this spot just right for resting from the day's rigorous events.

You'll also discover several large rocks in the creek that can easily accommodate those seeking prime seating for feasting on an impromptu picnic. You'll have little company as only a few cars can fit on this unpaved turnoff, and most people whizz by too quick to see this little cranny. It'll be on your right, about ten miles after exiting Lassen Park.

You'll have only 55 miles of roadway left once you reach the junction of Highways 89 and 299. These final miles are clearly geared for easy touring. An occasional little run of twisting, curving road will slip by, but for the most part, you'll now be treated to arrow-like straights through scenery that makes time pass much too quickly. Another treat for the traveler of Highway 89 is the views of Mt. Shasta on the last leg. Though about 50 miles away at first sighting, this snow-laden pinnacle adds a touch of class to an already illustrious set of memories.

This leisurely stretch of Highway 89 also makes it easy to enjoy the vast expanse of forest that shadows this area. Meadows and valleys, often utilized as grazing lands, liven up the scenery, too. Except for a few tiny communities spread along this final passage, there's little sign of civilization or traffic, though gas is available in most of these small towns.

The stretch from Cayton to Dead Horse Summit rises almost 1,500 feet in about 15 miles. Along much of this you'll find the elevation seesawing up and down. But even steeper inclines wait for you on the stretch from McCloud to McCloud Summit, as this section rises about 1,200 feet in only six miles. During the warm summer months, a watchful eye on the temperature gauge is recommended as it can get hot around this part of California.

Our trek on Highway 89 concludes at Interstate 5. Those who head south on Interstate 5 will find Mt. Shasta dancing in your rearview mirror as you scoot towards Redding. Streak north and you'll find Yreka, and further on, Oregon. The stretch of Interstate 5 radiating from the junction of Highway 89 has some of Interstate 5's best views. (Anyone who's traveled I-5 through Central California can tell you that interesting scenery is a rarity on this often boring north-south thoroughfare.)

You may have noticed that there are an inordinate number of turns necessary to stay on this highway. I assure you that all are clearly marked. You've also probably noticed that this road hooks up with plenty of other highways on its long journey through the hinterlands of Northeastern California. You'll get brief tastes of Highways 36, 44, 49, 50, and 70 before it's all over. (Highways 49 and 70 are both good roads and portions of the others are commendable.)

I find this road most soothing to the soul. In these modern times, we often forget what it's like to stand somewhere— anywhere—and not see any sign of man. This byway cuts through a part of the world that doesn't have to rely on billboards, bright lights, and loud noises to attract. With a path securely wrapped in tranquility and seclusion, Highway 89 represents a most magnificent matchup of scenery and pavement.

Highway 108

Direction: West.
Distance: About 80 miles.
Driving time: Three to five hours.
Congestion: Light, moderate around Sonora.
Road condition: Average early on, very good after that.
Patrol: Light, but heavy around Sonora.

Ah, the Sierra Nevada. This imposing mountain range runs over 350 miles from near Lassen Peak in Northern California down to Tejon Pass, 50 miles south of Bakersfield. To not include at least one highway that captures the grandeur of California's premier line of rugged peaks would be an injustice.

There's certainly no shortage of roads crossing over the Sierra Nevada. To the north lies Interstate 80. Though scenic for an Interstate, it offers little to the driving and riding enthusiast. Farther south is Highway 50, a popular road running from Sacramento to South Lake Tahoe. I excluded Highway 50 because it's heavily patrolled, and it offers little satisfaction in the fun-to-drive category.

Farther south courses Highway 120, a road with incredible scenery that runs through Yosemite National Park. But it's often a crowded and congested path, making fast, exciting motoring a near impossible feat.

So that leaves three serious contenders: Highways 4, 88, and 108. These three have several things in common: First, their best stretches run in an east-west direction, framed between Highways 49 and 395. Also, each is crowned with a high elevation summit that's closed by snow for much of the year. This trio also shares a similar texture, passing through lightly populated regions rimmed with beautiful forests and jagged mountain crests.

Let's first look at Highway 88, the northernmost of the troika. Starting in Nevada, this pleasant highway easily ranks as the most modern—and congested. And though its path is laced with great scenery, it doesn't offer quite the variety of Highways 4 and 108.

Next is Highway 4, our runner-up. If taken in an east-to-west direction, the first half of this mountain road dishes out plenty of wicked pavement for the driver. But for miles (too many miles for me), it meanders as a single lane, and fairly narrow one at that. The remainder of Highway 4—down the western side of the Sierra

134

Nevada—doesn't have the liveliness (or the curves and bends for that matter) that a good mountain ride needs to keep the serious driver and rider involved.

Don't get me wrong, the scenery on Highway 4 is attractive, with great vistas and lovely mountain lakes gracing its path. But when comparing these roads using all criteria, Highway 108 gets my nomination as the best route through the Sierra Nevada's granite peaks. Often accompanied by superb scenery, the enthusiast is sent on a winding course that's consistently fun and entertaining. Highway 108, from my experience, is also the least traveled of the three. And it's recently received expert resurfacing along much of its adventurous length.

This tour of Highway 108 begins on the steeper, eastern side of the Sierra Nevada, at Highway 395—in the middle of the Toiyabe Forest. To get to Highway 108 from South Lake Tahoe takes about an hour and a half using Highways 89 and 395. From the Reno, area, it's about 70 miles south along Highway 395.

One of the first things you're likely to notice as you settle in on Highway 108 is the snow. Even the warming effect of a long summer will leave pockets of snow still scattered about the landscape. For travelers coming off of the desert floor, it's an admittedly odd, yet refreshing sight.

Though mountains loom menacingly all around when starting out on Highway 108, you actually begin this trek snuggled securely in a broad valley that uses short straights and gentle, easy curves for transport. The road for the first five miles remains somewhat level, but serious climbing soon becomes the order of business as Highway 108 rises to an elevation of almost 10,000 feet within 15 miles.

After passing an out of place Marine training camp off to the right, you'll soon see the enthusiast's favorite road sign: "WINDING ROAD NEXT 24 MILES". The pretty Walker River will be on your left as the road begins to scale upwards. The road surface is about average on this incline, with minor bumps and broken pavement scattered here and there, letting you know in a polite way that this trail is not *that* far removed from being a back road. The smart motorist will keep an eye on the shoulder in the early going as it's crumbling in a few stretches.

Once you embark on the winding road section you'll find the center line performing a disappearing act, replaced with useless dabs of paint about every ten feet. There are few posted speed signs, but you'll probably take a lot of this in the 30-40 mph range. It's not tight, torturous stuff; rather the road simply lacks straights of any decent length.

The scenery on the first five miles of Highway 108 is not spectacular, but soon after Highway 108 lets loose with a barrage of appealing mountain scenes. Those who travel this road in the early morning will find a path that's quiet and serene, with little traffic to interfere with this westward journey. For those who will settle for nothing less than spectacular, the stretch of Highway 108 around Leavitt's Meadow—especially looking back towards the east—will easily fill the bill.

Passing Leavitt's Meadow brings a steep ascent that starts so high that even after dropping for a time, you're *still* mingling with mountain tops. The road coils occasionally, and in the higher elevations it can become a real handful as its squirrelly path attempts to dodge the bigger peaks. Approaching this piece of Highway 108 requires a respectful approach since this road's next step is always difficult to anticipate. Typically, you'll come flying out of a sharp, off-camber curve, expecting to be squeezed through an even more coiling path, only to find yourself facing a level quarter mile straight!

And the scenery of Highway 108 is just as surprising, treating you to an amazing array of sights. Looking like the colorful pages from a catalog one might use to furnish paradise, the views on this highway are impressive. Within an hour you'll discover an amazing collection of rock formations, meadows, rivers, waterfalls, snow banks, and more.

You'll also be treated to a dazzling display of color from a variety of wildflowers fighting for survival along this road. Blooming only when the weather turns warm for a few months every year, you'll see them waste little time as they burst out with all the colors of the rainbow, with no meadow or creekbed escaping the riotous bloom of yellows, purples, and pastels.

About fifteen miles into our journey we meet up with Sonora Pass at 9,624 feet. Only one other summit in California reaches a loftier point: Tioga Pass, about 35 miles south of Sonora Pass, with a summit of 9,941 feet. With over 8,000 feet between its high and low points, Highway 108 sends the enthusiast hurtling across the widest elevation range of any road listed here.

The road conditions improve considerably after leaving Sonora Pass. This section is full of interesting stretches marked by fast, well-banked curves and short, quick straights. And even though you'll be in an almost constant descent upon leaving the western flanks of the Sierra Nevada, Highway 108 offers little beyond Sonora Pass that's troublesome for the skilled driver and rider.

The striking scenery spread along Highway 108 is likely to slow all but the most intense enthusiast. And believe me, you wouldn't want to miss any of the incredible sights along this trek. At one memorable vista point, the vast Emigrant Wilderness stretches out towards the horizon in an unforgettable display of Mother Nature's creative abilities. Numerous spots exhort the traveler to stop; some have convenient information plaques posted, giving those of you with an interest, additional notes on what you're viewing.

At just under the 30 mile mark, you'll hit the small community of Dardanelle, where gas, food, and lodging are available. The 20 miles tucked between the towns of Dardanelle and Strawberry contain some of the most daring road, especially around the 35 mile mark. Coursing along asphalt in excellent condition, a bevy of medium to medium-tight curves can sometimes handcuff the nine-tenths enthusiast, making you feel like you're groping rather than motoring through this stellar collection of downward swirls. If you're unlucky enough to pickup traffic along this stretch, don't worry as you'll find an occasional straight, affording those with quick reflexes an opportunity to pass slower traffic.

The passage from Strawberry to Long Barn fills the terrain with solid forests of pine. Another valley, this time appearing off to the left, breaks up the thick forest walls before rising up to become Dodge Ridge. Just south of Peter Pam (don't ask) you'll find yourself on a divided highway—positively civilized—but still scenic, none-theless. But for a modern road, it's got a surprisingly curvy bent to its path. You'll lose the four-laner after a couple of miles, only to pick it up again just before the town of Twain Harte.

Between Long Barn and Twain Harte you'll say goodbye to the beautiful Stanislaus National Forest. Covering over a million acres, this scenic forest preserve is nature at its best. From Twain Harte until the end, travelers will find traffic heavier since this portion traverses a popular resort area.

Highway 108 now takes a more predictable path as it heads southeast towards our final destination of Sonora. And though this highway's contours will, on occasion, offer brief stretches where short little bursts are the order of the day, you'll find most of the final miles favoring sightseeing activities rather than the use of any highly refined driving and riding skills. But I assure you, as you travel along this forest-fringed trail, only the most hell-bent enthusiast will be disappointed with this road's overall package.

Heading into bustling Sonora, the realistic traveler should be prepared for heavy traffic most anytime of the day or week. The intersection in the middle of town can have especially long delays in store for the motorist. (Highway 49, also bringing traffic to this town, doesn't help matters any.) But Sonora is an interesting place; its history is full of delightful—if dubious—tales that skillfully blur fact with fiction. Gold was mined here (we're talking right in the streets, folks) mainly by Mexicans until they were driven out by

Americans evidently too lazy to find their own gold. If you can, save a little time for exploring this fascinating town.

As you continue moving off of the western slopes of the Sierra Nevada, the landscape begins a slow, yet constant tranformation from pine topped mountains to the brown foothills that are the scenic signature of the Gold Country. Those who wish to keep traveling along Highway 108—past our final destination of Sonora—will find it starting up again, a few miles south, off of Highway 49. From there, Highway 108 combines with Highway 120, dashing through the heart of the San Joaquin Valley before dying a slow death as a non-descript city street in lowly Modesto.

As I began collecting my thoughts for writing this road's summary, my mind kept drifting—not to the giant mountains and vast scenic vistas this road embraces, but to the wildflowers. And when I'm asked about this road, that is invariably what I end up rambling on about. In the mountainous regions of Highway 108, the roadside brims with a seemingly infinite variety of flowers; many with petals so delicate and fragile, you feel like you're witnessing some kind of miracle-in-progress; there they grow, in an environment frozen much of the year—bursting with color, with life, with determination.

You'll also find the landscape dotted with very young pine trees, many of them still seasons away from blending into the forest. I wonder about them too, as they appear so ill-equipped to deal with the always impending winter frost. Yet many survive, growing into bigger, stronger trees, faithfully replenishing what man and nature have taken.

Yes, this road will effectively feed the needs of just about any motoring enthusiast who desires a fast, challenging mountain course. Yet, Highway 108 also has a deeper character reflected in a vast collection of sights, smells, and sounds that one could easily miss if your attention is given only to its coiling, serpentine path. But after spending a day with this road, I think few travelers will remain untouched by this path's wonderful and satisfying traits.

Highway 128
and Pleasants Valley Rd

Direction: East.
Distance: About 50 miles.
Driving time: About two hours.
Congestion: Light to moderate.
Road condition: Very good.
Patrol: Light.

The region of Northern California known as the wine country continues to be a popular area for natives and tourists alike. And it's easy to see why. Blessed with great weather, beautiful scenery, famous vineyards, and an abundance of fine lodging and dining, it offers the traveler plenty of enjoyment. It would be a shame if a destination as interesting as the wine country didn't offer an exciting road in its selection of fun things to do. Well, we've joined together two great roads for your driving and riding pleasure, Highway 128 and Pleasants Valley Road.

This path gives the enthusiast an opportunity to discover the land lying just east of the wine country. It's beautiful canyon country, spotted with pristine lakes and cool streams. And the pavement that courses through it antes up almost 50 miles of smooth, open road. You'll find a lot of dips and twists pieced together with fast straights—all on well built roadway. This excursion offers a nice break from the hustle and bustle of the Napa Valley.

We begin our trek in the heart of the wine country in the small community of Rutherford, at the junction of Highways 29 and 128. Highway 29 is the main thoroughfare for the wine country, though Silverado Trail, running parallel about two miles east, is the easiest way to traverse the valley when in a hurry. If you're heading south on Highway 29, you'll need to make a left turn onto Highway 128; heading north, you'll turn right.

The first three miles pass through the eastern outskirts of Rutherford. Contained by a 35 mph speed limit, you'll drive on oak-lined streets passing lovely vineyards as you leisurely make your way to Silverado Trail. Make a right turn at Silverado Trail, and after about a hundred yards, make a left to continue on Highway 128.

After the left turn you'll begin to leave behind much of the congestion of the wine country. At this point, Highway 128 asks for a nimble approach as the well behaved pavement begins to disappear in your rearview mirror. You'll also notice the road narrowing considerably as the shoulder becomes smaller. But there's nothing *too* demanding in the early going as the road from Silverado Trail to the first sight of Lake Henessey consists mainly of slow-to-medium turns, with an occasional tight twist thrown in for good measure.

Lake Henessey acts much like a starting flag for a more challenging course. Commencing at about the five mile mark, the road follows the contours of this attractive lake, chalking up high marks in the fun-to-drive department.

As you leave Lake Henessey on a wide sweeper to the right, Highway 128 offers several new features. Just short of the seven mile mark, it introduces you to pretty Sage Creek, off to your right side. This marks the beginning of a nice set of fast-paced, yet easy to handle, lefts and rights best taken briskly. Short 100-200 foot straights allow you to build speed between these nicely banked curves.

Along this stretch, oak trees dominate the landscape. In winter and spring the hills are a beautiful shade of green; but the early part of the long California summers turn the surrounding foothills brown—then a golden yellow—as the hottest of seasons progresses. Midday temperatures can soar well into the 90's, especially in July and August.

Just past the seven mile mark, you'll have a mile of slightly hilly esses that can be most entertaining. The foothills move in closer—often just a stone's throw away. Luckily, you'll continue to have plenty of places to pull off and enjoy the countryside. Stop between the seven and nine mile marks and you'll hear the soft gurgling of Sage Creek, flowing just feet from Highway 128.

After a brief slalom just past the ten mile mark, you'll find the Nicelini Vineyard. For most, it functions more as a mileage marker than as a tourist destination (some recommendation, eh?). Sitting in the shadows of a pretty tree lined road, its small size makes it easy to miss.

Continuing past Nicelini Vineyard, Highway 128 provides a mixed bag of road for the next few miles. Discoveries include a short downhill slalom that flies through an attractive valley laden with grapes, shady groves, and open meadows.

Between the 15-20 mile mark there's plenty of straight road with a few easy curves thrown in for variety. It's a configuration that can promote high speeds; I've seen cars go over 90 mph on the straights that run through the valley that lies between Nicelini Vineyard and the junction of Highways 128 and 121.

Besides being the junction of Highways 128 and 121, the 19 mile mark is also home for the Monticello Restaurant. It's actually a combination small grocery store, deli, and restaurant. We often make this our breakfast stop when traveling early in the morning. It's not a fancy place. (It's actually a bit on the tacky side, with a decor that relies a little too much on plastic and vinyl.) But, its serves up great pancakes and good hot coffee, too. And if you don't want to sit at a table, just stroll up to the small counter, prop yourself up on one of the stools, and enjoy your meal there. For those lacking appetites, you can always rest outside under the shade trees on a couple of old weatherbeaten wooden chairs your grandparents might have owned twenty years back.

Moskowite Corner is the name given to the intersection where the Monticello Restaurant sits. Just a few feet away from our eating spot is the busy junction of Highways 128 and 121. You'll need to make a left turn to stay on Highway 128. After turning, you'll find the first three miles consist of gentle bends matched up with hilly straights. After several miles you'll encounter a few curves posted with 35 mph speed limits, effectively bringing your speed down.

Around 23 miles out, you'll see the turnoff for South Shore Resort. It also marks the beginning of an ascent that is the closest thing Highway 128 has to a mountain run. This incline greets you with a few switchbacks, plus a couple of tricky curves—all squeezed into an all-too-brief mile and a half surge to the summit. Canyon walls move much closer to the road, heightening the effect of this fun passage.

As you travel up and over this summit, your travels will take you through a long, narrow canyon where chaparral joins with a few trees to make up the vegetation that few would label nice. But the desolation is broken around 27 miles out by the Markley Cove Resort at Lake Berryessa. You can rent houseboats or do some fishing at this small resort tucked along the southern tip of Lake Berryessa. This pretty man-made lake offers a nice change of scenery. But, it also means additional traffic in the form of boat-lugging vehicles and campers. Lake Berryessa wil be your scenic companion for over two miles, until Monticello Dam. As the dam comes into sight on your left, you'll find a nice run of asphalt that uses brash little esses to find its way.

Leaving the lake behind, you'll head downwards where the final five miles of Highway 128 provide a good selection of hilly curves and bends, making aggressive driving seem almost mandatory. Leaving the more mountainous terrain, Highway 128 continues its enthusiastic ways as it moves southeast towards flatter ground. On this last stretch of Highway 128, you'll catch glimpses off to your right of what looks like a river, but is actually Solano Lake.

To get on the second leg of our trek, Pleasants Valley Road, just follow the sign that requires a right turn. The street sign will initially say Road 86, but it's just a short feeder road that quickly turns into Pleasants Valley Road. Within a mile the path begins a transformation into a charming country lane.

This fine back road, running a little over 12 miles, offers the traveler plenty of nice viewing. Lovely horse farms and blooming fruit orchards join with an array of images one only seems to find these days on a pastoral lane like Pleasants Valley Road.

As this road unfolds, you'll be charmed by its white picket fences and its friendly, free running, tail-wagging dogs; all add to this lane's captivating character. Beautiful, yet understated houses dispersed along the way add their effect to this delightful back road, too.

Pleasants Valley Road also provides the driving and riding enthusiast with a nice range of road to stretch out on. You'll find the most demanding sections of this narrow two-lane well dispersed along its path. With a judicious use of warning and speed limit signs, this road advertises all of the tough stuff in advance, making it easy to quickly get a feel for the lay of this road.

It fits my driving personality very well; always coming up with a nice straight just when the twisty stuff gets a bit tiresome. In general, Pleasants Valley Road is much flatter than Highway 128, but that seems to have little effect on the fun nature of this road.

The last curve of Pleasants Valley Road curls to the left, readying you for one last straight. At its end, you'll meet up with Interstate 80 and head either northeast, towards Sacramento, or aim southwest, towards Oakland and San Francisco. Please note: if you decide to run these two roads in the opposite direction—beginning at Interstate 80—you'll need to get off Interstate 80 at the Cherry Glen Road exit, make a right turn, and you're on Pleasants Valley Road.

Both Highway 128 and Pleasants Valley Road are in very good condition. Much of Highway 128 rides like a dream, with only an occasional small rockslide (warnings posted) marring its excellent condition. Pleasants Valley Road is also in good shape—keeping in mind that it's a lightly traveled back road that's not high on the road maintenance list.

Traffic can be a different story, especially on Highway 128. The numerous recreational facilities that lie along its path draw a lot of visitors, but rarely is the traffic oppressive. The worst spots are around Lake Berryessa and Moskowite Corner. Get through these two areas and you'll generally find open road with few exceptions. Congestion will rarely be a problem on Pleasants Valley Road. In addition, patrol is usually light on both roads, though rarely nonexistent.

Every year, I spend at least a couple of long weekends in the wine country. For years my favorite place to relax has been the Harvest Inn, located in St. Helena. The owner, Richard Geyer, has tastefully furnished his rooms and cottages with beautiful antiques, complete with touches of brass and oak. Its warm and friendly staff makes this a most comfortable place to stay. And the lovingly tended grounds always have numerous flowers and plants in full bloom.

Set alongside a working vineyard, breakfast on the patio at the Harvest Inn (often with Richard in attendance) is a treat I always look forward to. Richard's tales of his never ending battles with the local government and zoning officals will leave you laughing and crying at the same time. I like this place and I highly recommend it. Due to its popularity, the Harvest Inn has grown considerably over the years. But I assure you, that with Richard's guiding hand, no matter how big it gets, this lovely retreat will never lose its tranquil atmosphere.

So there you have it. An itinerary consisting of two great car roads, a lovely inn, tasty pancakes—all sitting in one of the most beautiful regions of California. I try to visit in the spring or late fall as the crowds and prices tend to be more bearable. But no matter when you go, Highway 128 and Pleasants Valley Road will be waiting, offering the traveler year-round enjoyment.

Highway 299

Direction: East.
Distance: About 140 miles.
Driving time: From three to five hours.
Congestion: Light, moderate at each end.
Road condition: Good condition.
Patrol: Light.

This road trip is an outing that offers splendid scenery, much of it residing within the confines of Six Rivers National Forest. It also provides the enthusiast with a goodly amount of thrills as it cuts an easterly path through the forested western slopes of California's rugged coastal range. Running from near the Pacific Ocean, inland to Redding and Interstate 5, this road's fine views and fast, smooth pavement make for a most enjoyable journey.

Highway 299 holds several scenic diversions sure to brighten your path. Both Whiskeytown Lake and the historic community of Weaverville offer the traveler the opportunity for adventure. In addition, sporting types can look forward to stretches of outstanding asphalt that are sure to enthrall any fan of curvacious road. Throw in four major summits ranging from 2,262 feet to 3,215 feet, and you've got a road course guaranteed to reward those deft behind the wheel.

We launch this excursion near Eureka, where our featured road originates. You'll find the exit for Highway 299 on Highway 101, about 12 miles north of Eureka. Most travelers will be glad to abandon the forboding cold and fog that permeate this section of California coastline for the more temperate environs inland. Even the warmth of summer can't seem to rid this area of its often dismal weather.

Highway 299 begins by mimicking a four-lane freeway, which, as explained later, can improve the initial miles on this roadway. Though the first five miles of scenery aren't world class, the views quickly improve as you take aim towards a seemingly endless forest of evergreens.

You'll begin climbing just past the small hamlet of Blue Lake. Timely passing lanes—masquerading as a second lane each way—are thoughtfully placed throughout this incline, making the traffic seem lighter than it really is. These passing alleys come in handy since plenty of campers and logging trucks use Highway 299. With logging and tourism ranking as two of the major *legal* industries in this area, you'd expect no less, right?

144

Lord-Ellis Summit, about 17 miles into the trip, is the first high mark at 2,262 feet. Up to this point, the road has been a leisurely cruise, built for speed on smooth, well behaved sweepers. Warm weather induces a variety of colorful wildflowers to spring up along this passage, adding to what is already a section laced with fine scenery.

Moving east from the Lord-Ellis Summit, the forests thicken and the passage is distinguished by travel through several beautiful valleys. Thankfully, this road provides numerous opportunities to pull off the pavement, though few of the turnouts are paved. In the first half of our journey, the best vantage spot sits near the 27 mile point, marked with a sign reading, "VISTA POINT 1 MILE". This large turnoff offers a panoramic overview of some of the coiled pavement just frequented.

About a half mile past the vista point is a second crest, Berry Summit, at an elevation of 2,859 feet. Around this location, the road becomes a tighter course with bends and twists coming with greater frequency. Narrowing at times, there's still nothing too harrowing for those commanding even a smidgen of skill.

A mile after Berry Summit, a delightful, albeit, brief series of esses await the enthusiast. The canyon walls close in a bit—heightening the effect of feeling like you're scrambling along some long forgotten back road. Continuing east, your descent steepens, toppling a dizzying 2,100 in the seven miles since Berry Summit, certainly not hurting this road's fun-to-drive rating. This twisting pavement's angled approach grabs you by the collar, making sure that your attention is firmly affixed to the asphalt ahead.

Another great dash awaits you on the stretch of pavement just before the small town of Willow Creek, about 40 miles into our trip. But I'm sorry to report that as you near Willow Creek, traffic will usually thicken. Upon leaving civilization, there are several straights long enough to provide you with the option to pass vehicles in front of you.

You'll cross the boundary of Six Rivers National Forest just before Willow Creek. Though much of this 1.1 million acre forest is only accessible on foot or horseback, Highway 299 does a more than respectable job as tour guide, yielding a good look at this lovely area.

Rather than stop in Willow Creek like most people, I continue on to a little rest stop about ten minutes east of town. It seems that most travelers pass the Salyer rest stop by, and that's fine with me. That means I've got a better chance of nabbing one of the prime parking spots underneath the pine trees shading this quiet place. Though on the small side as highway rest stops go, Salyer comes equipped with picnic benches and a place for your pet to take care of business. (Now there's a crazy thought: I can hear the enthusiast screaming to his poodle strapped to the front seat, "Hey, Todd, here comes another bunch of cool curves, we'll stop later, okay little buddy?") The rest rooms are always clean here too, making it easy to give this roadside rest high marks.

Upon exiting the rest stop, passing lanes appear, simplifying the act of putting open road in front of you. And all the better, because you'll soon encounter esses that *look* fantastic. They're just over a rise, about a mile and a half past the rest stop. The first time I spied these stunning curves, all that seemed missing was a gilded picture frame and the signature of the designing engineer in the lower corner! Though lasting less than a minute, the moment you see these curvaceous works of art, a smile is sure to appear on your face. (And, yes, they're as fun to take as they are to gaze upon.)

Upon leaving Willow Creek, Highway 299 joins up with the Trinity River, though it's difficult to see initially since it's flowing hundreds of feet below the road. Eventually, the road bustles downwards, closing in on the river's banks as it streaks onward in a southeasterly direction.

Once you shimmy up to this river's contours, the real fireworks begin. Here, with the Trinity River on your left, is where the enthusiast can get on with some serious driving and riding. Encouraged by this tributary's scroll-like path, this outing certainly has the potential to bring aggressive types into intimate contact with their own limits. Along this stretch, you'll need more than a firm grip to outwit the rambunctious pavement that lies in wait.

After traveling with the Trinity River for nearly 12 miles, the William B. Abbar Bridge escorts you over the water and sets you gently down so the Trinity River is now to your right. From here, many will notice an easing in the way this road careems through these mountains as it trys in vain to keep up with the river's course.

Another welcome change on this part of Highway 299 is the flattening of the road—an agreeable trend considering the seemingly endless ascents and descents of the first 50 miles. Finally, views of the lovely Trinity River become a prime source of scenery. Highway 299—now running close to its rocky banks—is often less than 20 feet away. You'll lose this stream on occasion (like at Del Loma), but you'll return to its side, usually just a brief moment after parting company. At times, the Trinity River spans over 50 feet; while other times it's but a trickle. And you won't see many people on it, as the stretch you're traveling isn't that good for rafting. Those looking to stop to enjoy the pleasant views along this section of Highway 299 should have little problem in finding a consenting shoulder to pull off on.

From Del Loma to the turnoff for Junction City is about 21 miles, most of it continuing to merrily flow along a path carved out by the Trinity River. Nearing Junction City, you'll part company with this lovely watercourse, with Highway 299 going east while the river flows south. The road begins to change character as it adapts to losing the serpentine-like influence of the Trinity River. The ground-work becomes somewhat straighter, now making fewer demands upon the driver and rider.

The road on the Del Loma—Junction City leg holds several straights long enough to allow you to pass most of the campers and logging rigs that might have accumulated in front of you. You'll find plenty of interesting road, similar to the pavement before Del Loma, though maybe not as twisting as some enthusiasts would like. The lovely scenery on this portion seldom varies, blending scenic water-ways with dense forests of pine and fir into a terrific exhibition of nature's beauty.

From Junction City, travelers are whisked to the next community in just a few minutes. Weaverville, about 90 miles into our trip, is easily the most interesting town along Highway 299. Retaining much of the color and atmosphere of the old gold mining days, you can still pan for the glittery flakes and nuggets in these parts. This bustling town of about 3,000 friendly people is loaded with charm. I always try to spend time visiting some of the quaint shops and businesses along Main Street—which also happens to be Highway 299.

The first ten miles of asphalt past Weaverville, though hilly, hold little challenge. Typical on this stretch are half mile straights joined with high gear sweepers. Since leaving town, you've traveled in a southerly direction, but soon you'll move east, coming into contact with your old sidekick, the Trinity River.

For those who've collected slower traffic in front of them, there's another passing lane about ten miles out of Weaverville. And, with the highway getting steep, plus an often moderate amount of traffic on this last segment, the passing lane is likely to prove indispensible. After you've completed your passing duties, the road cracks down-wards, only to soon after move upwards again.

From Weaverville, the terrain gives but a modest amount of input into the lay of the highway. But at Buckhorn Summit that mild influence quickly turns into a rage. Here, the hills begin to buck under the road like a wild bull—sculpting pavement that's guaranteed to delight.

The finest stretch of Highway 299 begins as the road hurtles you over a crest of 3,215 feet, about 20 miles past Weaverville. These eight miles—almost completely downhill—represent the best course you can wring out of this roadway. Tumbling quickly out of the mountains, it throws countless turns, twists, and switchbacks at you as it cuts its steep path with wild abandon. There are so many nasty curves on this angled run that any showing of them would have to be rated X. At its best, it's downright hair-raising; at its worst, it presents plenty of plunging, off-camber paving that can generate numerous opportunities for high drama. Buckhorn Run is the nickname we've given this last serious piece of driving on Highway 299.

Finishing off this arresting downhill run, the road levels and straightens out, which might leave the diehard road fan feeling a bit glum. Well, your spirits are sure to be lifted anew with the sighting of Whiskeytown Lake—certainly one of the prettier man-made bodies of water in California. This scenic delight comes into view just as you're catching your breath from the drop off of the summit. As part of the Whiskeytown-Shasta-Trinity National Recreation area, you'll often see this lovely lake dotted with boaters and water skiers. If you wish to stop, there's a vista point on the right, just as you begin to put the lake behind you.

The last seven or so miles into Redding are fairly uneventful. Congestion increases as you close in on your final destination. This trek ends unceremoniously in the middle of bustling downtown Redding. Those intent on connecting with Interstate 5 will find signs clearly showing the way.

Highway 299, linking the coast with the northernmost section of California's fertile central valley, is a much quicker route than its older sister road to the south, Highway 36 (also in this guide). Highway 299, the more modern of the two, takes less time, but still pays ample dividends in the scenery and driving departments.

Extensive work on Highway 299's surface has left many of its miles as smooth as glass. As other portions of this route receive attention, you're likely to encounter road work in progress, but little should be so extensive as to slow your passage. Another plus is that patrol is fairly light on most of this trek, though you'll usually see the CHP at least once, especially on the eastern portions of this byway.

One word of caution: plenty of logging trucks use this road, especially during the weekdays. These big rigs constantly exceed the speed limit, taking curves way too fast, always taking some of the opposite lane with them—as if they were on a one-way (their way) road.

While it has a lot going for it, Highway 299 is not the perfect path. While blessed with fine scenery, the view changes little for much of Highway 299's 140 miles. In addition, serious enthusiasts probably realize that most of Highway 299 does not consist of mile-after-mile of hard-core, death defying road. It certainly has some great twitches of pavement (Buckhorn Run!), but much of it is better suited to touring than heart-thumping sport. This is especially true of the first 20 miles of this road. I heartily encourage you to give this road a try, as I think most enthusiasts will delight in Highway 299's ability to wrap a reasonably entertaining range of driving and riding experiences into its length.

APPENDIX

Getting a ticket in California

So, here you are from another state, traveling in California, and you get a moving violation. Will the information be transferred to your driving record back in your home state? The following states receive information from California, as members of the National Driver License Compact.

Alabama	Mississippi
Arizona	Montana
Arkansas	Nebraska
Colorado	Nevada
Delaware	New Jersey
Florida	New Mexico
Hawaii	New York
Idaho	Oklahoma
Illinois	Oregon
Indiana	Tennessee
Iowa	Utah
Kansas	Virginia
Louisiana	Washington
Maine	West Virginia

California Highway Information Network

Now here's a nifty idea: a network of phone numbers throughout California that gives travelers pre-recorded messages on current road conditions, including updates on weather and construction delays. In the past, the system was plagued with low quality recordings that were often unintelligible. But new equipment installed in early 1988 should alleviate that problem, plus give the system greater flexibility.

Angels Camp . . . . (209) 736-4564
Auburn . . . . (916) 885-3786
Bakersfield . . . . (805) 393-1582 (north)
Bakersfield . . . . (805) 393-7350 (south)
Bishop . . . . (619) 873-6366

```
Chico................(916) 895-8111
Eureka...............(707) 444-3077
Fresno...............(209) 227-7264
Grass Valley.........(916) 272-2171
Jackson..............(209) 223-4455

Los Angeles..........(213) 626-7231
Marysville...........(916) 743-4681
Merced...............(209) 383-4291
Modesto..............(209) 521-2240
Newhall..............(805) 259-8081

Oakland..............(415) 654-9890
Oroville.............(916) 534-7900
Placerville..........(916) 622-7355
Quincy...............(916) 283-1045
Redding..............(916) 244-1500

Riverside............(714) 788-7600
Sacramento...........(916) 445-7623
Salinas..............(408) 757-2006
San Bernardino.......(714) 888-6501
San Francisco........(415) 557-3755

San Jose.............(408) 436-1404
San Luis Obispo......(805) 543-1985 (north)
San Luis Obispo......(805) 543-9544 (south)
Santa Ana............(714) 972-9980
Santa Rosa...........(707) 585-0326

South Lake Tahoe.....(916) 577-3550
Sonora...............(209) 532-0227
Stockton.............(209) 931-4848
Susanville...........(916) 257-5126
Ukiah................(707) 462-0155

Vallejo..............(707) 643-8421
Ventura..............(805) 653-1821
Walnut Creek.........(415) 938-1180
Yreka................(916) 842-1217
```

Source: Department of Transportation

65 mph speed limit

As of January, 1988, there are 1,157 miles of rural California Interstates posted with the 65 mph speed limit.

Interstate 5 (473 miles)
- Starting at Bakersfield at Highway 99 and running to Roth Rd., just south of Stockton.
- It begins again just north of Stockton one mile north of Hammer Lane continuing until just south of Sacramento.
- It continues from the Yolo Bypass Bridge to Dunsmuir.
- From Dunsmuir to less than a mile from the Oregon border.

Interstate 8 (133 miles)
- From Flinn Springs near El Cajon to the Mica Gem Undercrossing.
- Picking up again near Octillo at Route 98 and continuing east until about two miles from the Arizona border.

Interstate 10 (154 miles)
- From Calimesa Blvd. in Beaumont to the Arizona border.

Interstate 15 (181 miles)
- From Deer Springs Rd. near Escondido into Riverside county, ending at Glen Ivy.
- Picking up again just south of Kenwood Ave., near San Bernardino until reaching the East Baker Overcrossing.
- The last five miles before the Nevada border.

Interstate 40 (155 miles)
- From Barstow to the Arizona border.

Interstate 205 (13 miles)
- From Interstate 580 until reaching Interstate 5.

Interstate 505 (33 miles)
- From Route 80 near Vacaville to Interstate 5.

Interstate 580 (16 miles)
- From Interstate 5 to Interstate 205.

Source: California Highway Patrol

Driving Schools

Here's a sampling of some of the better known driving schools that offer the automobile enthusiast a chance to improve their driving skills. All hold training courses at various California racetracks at regular intervals. All fees listed are subject to change.

Bob Boundurant School of High Performance Driving.
Sears Point International Raceway
Highways 37 & 121
Sonoma, CA. 95476
(707) 938-4741

These folks have everything from a giant skid pad to a accident simulator. Small classes. One-day advanced street driving course covers basic car control, evasive maneuvers, skid control and more. If you use your own car, you'll need $325 to get into this course.

Jim Russell Racing Drivers School
Laguna Seca Raceway
1023 Salinas-Monterey Highway
Salinas, CA 93908
1-800-821-8755 (outside of California)
1-800-422-8867 (California)

Okay, Okay, these guys don't exactly offer an advanced street driving course, but they'll provide training that'll make you one darn good racer if your goal is to get started in IMSA or SCCA events. But if you're not a better street driver after spending nearly two grand on their three day Techniques of Driving racing course, then you ought to give up driving. Courses use Formula Fords.

Porsche Precision Driving School with Derek Bell
Derek Bell Motorsports, Inc.
P.O. Box 11912
Ft. Lauderdale, Fl. 33339
(305) 561-2881

This one day precision driving course, new in 1988, covers many of the fundamental techniques needed to become a better driver. Wiliow Springs seems to be the track of choice. Porsche had a hand in getting this started, so many of your classmates will be driving Porsches ($550.00 for this course).

Skip Barber Racing/Advanced Driving School
Route 7
Canaan, Ct. 06018
(203) 824-0771

Using BMW 3 and 5 series models, you'll get a choice of a one day ($400) or two day ($700) course that can help refine and heighten your driving abilities. Includes skidpad, auto cross, accident evasion simulator, and more.

INDEX

ABOUT THE AUTHOR

   After retiring at the age of two from car sales due to strict child labor laws and an acute bow tie shortage, the author was taken against his will by larger people to California.

   Stints as a middle manager at a Fortune 50 company, manager of a hot dog stand in Berkeley, electronic music composer in Hollywood, and numerous advertising and writing projects have left him slightly odd. Currently living in a small beach community somewhere in California, he valiantly continues his struggle against adulthood.

   This book is considered therapy.

ORDER FORM

Need another copy of *The Best Roads of California?*
Want to send a copy to another enthusiast
as a gift?
Like to have an additional full color map
(11x17) of California's best roads?

Send me _____ copy(s) of *The Best Roads of California* (includes color map) at $15.95 each ($13.95 plus $2.00 postage/handling.)

Send me _____ full color (11x17) map(s) of California's best roads at $3.50 each. ($2.50 plus $1.00 postage/handling.)

Total amount enclosed: $ _____

Send to: Name: _____
            Street: _____
            City, State, Zip: _____

☐ This is a gift, send to _____
_____
_____

We'll include a card noting you as the giver. If you would like an additional message on the card let us know:
_____
_____
_____

Send to: RoadTales Publishing
            P.O. Box 30218
            Long Beach. CA 90853